CHRIST THE HEALER

CHRIST THE HEALER

F.F. Bosworth

Whitaker House

Editor's note: This book has been edited for the modern reader. Words, expressions, and sentence structure have been updated for clarity and readability.

CHRIST THE HEALER

ISBN: 0-88368-591-4
Printed in the United States of America
© 2000 by Whitaker House

Whitaker House
30 Hunt Valley Circle
New Kensington, PA 15068

Library of Congress Cataloging-in-Publication Data

Bosworth, F. F. (Fred Francis), 1877–1958.
    Christ the Healer / by F. F. Bosworth
        p. cm.
    Includes bibliographical references.
    ISBN 0-88368-591-4 (pbk.)
    1. Spiritual Healing. I. Title.
BT732.5 .B67 2000
234'.131—dc21   00-009171

3 4 5 6 7 8 9 10 11 12 / 09 08 07 06 05 04 03 02

CONTENTS
✦

Author's Note to the Reader

If you have been taught to regard sickness as a *"thorn in the flesh"* (2 Cor. 12:7) that must remain, I would urge you to read chapter six, "What Was Paul's 'Thorn'?" before you read any other chapter in this book. Otherwise, you will likely miss the force of the scriptural arguments presented in other parts of the book.

One

✦

Does Jesus' Atonement
Include Healing?

One

✦

Does Jesus' Atonement Include Healing?

Before giving a biblical answer to the question, Does Jesus' atonement include healing? I invite your attention to a few facts taught in the Scriptures that pertain to this subject.

The Scriptures declare, in Romans 5:12, that *"by one man sin entered into the world, **and death by sin"*** (emphasis added). Here it is plainly stated that death entered the world through sin. Therefore, it is clear that disease, which is incipient death, entered into the world by sin. Now, since disease entered by sin, its true remedy must be found in the redemption of Christ. Since disease reached us through the power of Satan—and the Scriptures call disease the oppression of the Devil (Acts 10:38)—what power, when nature fails, can remove it but the power of the Son of God?

As soon as disease has advanced beyond the power of nature to restore us, it will result in death in every case unless removed by the power of God. All honest physicians will admit this, for they claim only the power to assist nature, not to heal. In this event, anything that would hinder the power of God from supplementing nature would make recovery impossible.

Accordingly, James said, *"Confess your faults one to another...that ye may be healed"* (James 5:16)—meaning that, otherwise, you cannot be healed.

When disease has advanced beyond the power of nature, neither nature, nor the physician, nor even prayer can save the sufferer until he confesses his sins—unless God, for some sovereign purpose of His own, removes the disease. Since disease is a part of the Curse, its true remedy must be the Cross, for who can remove the Curse but God, and how can God *justly* do it except by substitution? The Bible teaches, as one writer put it, that disease is the physical penalty of iniquity, but that Christ has borne in His body all our physical liabilities on account of sin, and that therefore our bodies are released judicially from disease.

Through Christ's redemption, we may all have, as a part of the *"earnest* ["*guarantee*," NKJV] *of our inheritance"* (Eph. 1:14), the *"life also of Jesus...manifest in our mortal flesh"* (2 Cor. 4:11) to supplement nature until our work is finished. In the same way that we may receive the *"firstfruits"* (Rom. 8:23) of our spiritual salvation, we can receive the *"firstfruits"* of our physical salvation.

Did Jesus Redeem Us from Our Diseases?

Now, to the question: Did Jesus redeem us from our diseases when He atoned for our sins?

If, as some teach, healing is not in the Atonement, why were types of the Atonement given in connection with bodily healing throughout the Old Testament? In the twelfth chapter of Exodus, why were the Israelites required to eat the flesh of the Passover lamb for physical strength, unless it was to show that we can receive physical life, or strength, from Christ, who, Paul said, is *"our passover...sacrificed for us"* (1 Cor. 5:7)? Seven hundred sixty-five years after the institution of the Passover, we read in 2 Chronicles 30:20 that *"the LORD hearkened to Hezekiah, and healed the people"* when they kept the Passover. Accordingly, Paul, in 1 Corinthians 11:29, spoke of the failure of the Corinthians to rightly *"understand the body"* (WEYMOUTH) of *"Christ our passover"* (1 Cor. 5:7) as the reason why many among them were *"weak and sickly"* (1 Cor. 11:30).

The Lord's Supper is more than an ordinance, because we may partake of Christ while we are partaking of the emblems of His death and the benefits thereof. In Christ there is both bodily and spiritual life, and surely there is no better time for availing ourselves of the privilege of having the *"life also of Jesus ...manifest in our mortal flesh"* (2 Cor. 4:11).

Healing Taught in Old Testament Types

Again, in Leviticus 14:18, we read of the priest making atonement for the cleansing of the leper. Why an atonement for the leper's healing if healing for us is not in the Atonement of Christ? The types in the fourteenth and fifteenth chapters of Leviticus show us that it was invariably through atonement that sickness was healed. This, to my mind, is a complete answer to the question we are discussing, should we go no further, because all of these typical atonements point to and prefigure Calvary.

Again, Jesus told us, in Luke 4:19, that He was anointed *"to preach the acceptable year of the LORD,"* referring to the Old Testament Year of Jubilee. This shows us that the Year of Jubilee is strikingly typical of Gospel blessings, for here He Himself applies the Year of Jubilee to the Gospel era.

Leviticus 25:9 shows us that no blessing of the Year of Jubilee was to be announced by the sounding of the trumpet until the Day of Atonement. On this Day, a young bull was slain as a sin offering, and the mercy seat was sprinkled with blood. No mercy was offered until the blood of the atonement sprinkled the mercy seat, because it would be a judgment seat if not sprinkled with blood. This teaches us that no mercy or blessing of the Gospel is offered to us irrespective of Christ's atonement.

Recovery of Everything Lost in the Fall

Through the Fall, we lost everything. Jesus recovered it all through His atonement. God said that, on the Day of Atonement, *"ye shall return every man unto his possession"* (Lev. 25:10). The order in the Year of Jubilee was this: *first,* the atonement, *then,* the sounding of the trumpet of the Jubilee, with the glad tidings, *"Ye shall return every man unto his possession."* Likewise, the order is the same now: first, Calvary, then, the Gospel trumpet that He *"bare our sins"* (1 Pet. 2:24), *"bare our sicknesses"* (Matt. 8:17), and so on, to be sounded *"to every creature"* (Mark 16:15), showing us that we may *"return every man unto his possession."*

God's seven redemptive names, one of which is JEHOVAH-RAPHA, which means, *"I am the LORD that healeth thee"* (Exod. 15:26), show us what lost possessions each of us may return to during our dispensation. The two outstanding possessions to be restored during the Gospel era are health for soul and body; therefore, forgiveness and healing were offered universally wherever Christ preached *"the acceptable year of the Lord"* (Luke 4:19), in order that the inner and outer man might be whole and ready for the service of God, *"thoroughly furnished unto all good works"* (2 Tim. 3:17) so they could finish their course.

Some of the fundamentalists who attack the Christian Scientists for believing we can be saved irrespective of Calvary make exactly the same blunder when they say they believe in healing but that it is offered irrespective of Calvary. It is to me, as well as to them, a mystery how anyone can say that the blood of Christ was just as effective flowing in His veins as it was when it was shed, in the face of every bleeding sacrifice of the Old Testament to the contrary, and also the statement, *"Without shedding of blood is no remission* [of sins]" (Heb. 9:22).

Adopt a bloodless religion, and you have but a religion of ideas, and nothing but a human thrill, because *"joy unspeakable and full of glory"* (1 Pet. 1:8) can never be known except by those who have been saved through the blood of Christ. It is just as great a mystery to me how these fundamentalists can say that healing is bestowed without reference to Christ's death. The salvation of any part of man without sacrifice is unknown in Scripture.

If bodily healing is offered and is to be preached regardless of Calvary, why was it that no blessing of the Year of Jubilee was to be announced by the sounding of the trumpet until the Day of Atonement? Paul told us that it is in Christ that all the promises of God are *"yea"* and *"Amen"* (2 Cor. 1:20), which is another way of saying that all the promises of God, including His promise to heal, owe their existence and power exclusively to the redeeming work of Christ.

Healing Not Deferred until the Millennium

Some ministers are trying to relegate bodily healing to the millennial day, but Jesus said, *"This day* [not the millennial day] *is this scripture fulfilled in your ears"* (Luke 4:21). It was in the church (not the Millennium) that God appointed teachers, miracles, gifts of healings, and so on (1 Cor. 12:28). None in the church will need healing during the Millennium, because they will receive glorified bodies before the Millennium, when they are *"caught up...to meet the Lord in the air"* (1 Thess. 4:17), when what is mortal puts on immortality (1 Cor. 15:53–54). If we are going to relegate healing to the Millennium, we will also have to do so with the teachers and so on that God appointed in the church, along with the gifts of healings. To say that healing is only for the Millennium is synonymous with saying that we are now in the Millennium, because God is healing many thousands in this day.

God's all-inclusive promise is to pour His Spirit upon all flesh (Joel 2:28) during *"the acceptable year of the Lord"* (Luke 4:19), which is the dispensation of the Holy Spirit. He comes as Christ's executive, to execute for us all the blessings of redemption—to bring to us *"the earnest* [*"guarantee,"* NKJV]*"* (Eph. 1:14) or *"firstfruits"* (Rom. 8:23) of our spiritual and physical inheritance, until the last enemy, which is death, is destroyed (1 Cor. 15:26), thus admitting us to our full inheritance.

Faith Comes by Hearing

The reason why many of the sick in our day have not returned to their physical possessions is that they have not heard the trumpet sound on this line. *"Faith*

Does Jesus' Atonement Include Healing? ✦

cometh by hearing" (Rom. 10:17), and they have not heard because many ministers had their Gospel trumpet put out of order while they were in theological seminary. They remind me of a man whom I knew who played a trombone in a brass band. At the beginning of a rehearsal, the boys put a small spike into the mouthpiece of his horn, so that, when he blew, his breath went against the head of the spike, making it impossible for him to produce much sound out of the horn; but he went through the whole rehearsal without discovering what was wrong. Some preachers, like this man, think they are blowing their Gospel trumpet all right, and have not discovered that there is not half as much coming out of it as there ought to be. They are not, like Paul, declaring *"all the counsel of God"* (Acts 20:27).

As in Leviticus the types show that healing was invariably through atonement, so Matthew 8:16–17 definitely states that Christ healed all diseases on the ground of the Atonement. The Atonement was His reason for making no exceptions while healing the sick: *"He...healed all that were sick: that it might be fulfilled which was spoken by Esaias* [Isaiah] *the prophet, saying, Himself took our infirmities, and bare our sicknesses."* Since it is *our* sicknesses He bore, His atonement embracing us all, it would require the healing of all to fulfill this prophecy. Jesus is still healing all who come to Him with living faith, *"that it might be fulfilled...."*

Since, in the darker age of the types, all the people had the privilege of being healed, surely in this "better" dispensation, with its *"better covenant"* and *"better promises"* (Heb. 8:6), God has not withdrawn this Old Testament mercy. If so, we are robbed that much by the coming and atonement of Christ.

In Numbers 16:46–50, after 14,700 of the Israelites had died of the plague, Aaron, as priest, in his mediatorial office, stood for the people between the dead and the living and made an atonement for the removal of the plague—the healing of the body. In the same way, Christ, our Mediator, by His atonement, redeemed us from the "plague" of sin and sickness.

The Type of the Bronze Serpent

In Numbers 21:9, we read of the Israelites all being healed by looking at the bronze serpent, which was lifted up as a type of the Atonement (John 3:14). If healing was not to be in the Atonement, why were these dying Israelites required to look at the *type* of the Atonement for bodily healing? Since both healing and forgiveness came through the type of the Atonement, why not to us through Christ, the Antitype? As their curse was removed by the lifting up of the bronze serpent, so Paul told us that ours is removed by the lifting up of Christ (Gal. 3:13).

In Job 33:24–25, we read: *"I have found a ransom* [atonement, *Scofield Reference Bible,* margin]. *His flesh shall be fresher than a child's: he shall return to the days of his youth."* Here, we see that Job's flesh was healed through an atonement. Why not ours?

David opened Psalm 103 by calling upon his soul to bless the Lord and to *"forget not all his benefits"* (v. 2); and then he specified, *"Who forgiveth all thine iniquities; who healeth all thy diseases"* (v. 3). How does God forgive sin? Of course, through the atonement of Christ. He heals disease in the same way, because the atonement of Jesus Christ is the only ground for any benefit to fallen man. How can God save any part of man except through the Atonement?

In 1 Corinthians 10:11, Paul told us, *"All these things happened unto them for ensamples* [types]: *and they are written for our admonition, upon whom the ends of the world are come."* In Galatians 3, the Holy Spirit shows us clearly that these things are for us as well as for Israel.

> *Know ye therefore that they which are of faith, the same are the children of Abraham....Now to Abraham and his seed were the promises made....And if ye* [Gentiles] *be Christ's, then are ye Abraham's seed, and heirs according to the promise.* (Gal. 3:7, 16, 29)

"Now therefore ye are no more strangers and foreigners, but fellowcitizens with the saints, and of the household of God" (Eph. 2:19).

The Reverend Daniel Bryant, in his book *Christ among Our Sick,* said,

> The church then learned what the church needs, it seems, to learn again; namely, that there is no difference to the compassionate Christ between a sick Gentile and a sick Jew.

The Seven Redemptive Names of Jehovah

To me, another unanswerable argument that healing is in the Atonement is to be found in the seven redemptive names of Jehovah. Mr. Scofield, in his footnote on Exodus 34:6 in the *Scofield Reference Bible* on the redemptive names, said that the name "Jehovah is distinctly the redemption name of Deity," and means "the self-existent One" who reveals Himself. These seven redemptive names, he said, "point to a continuous and increasing self-revelation." He then said, "In His redemptive relation to man, Jehovah has seven compound names which reveal Him as meeting every need of man from his lost state to the end."

Since it is His redemptive relationship to us that these names reveal, they must each point to Calvary where we were redeemed, and the blessing that each name reveals must be provided by the Atonement. This the Scriptures clearly teach.

The following are the seven redemptive names:

JEHOVAH-SHAMMAH, *"The LORD is there"* (Ezek. 48:35), or present, reveals to us the redemptive privilege of enjoying the presence of the One who says, *"Lo, I am with you alway"* (Matt. 28:20). That this blessing is provided by the Atonement is proven by the fact that we *"are made nigh by the **blood** of Christ"* (Eph. 2:13, emphasis added).

JEHOVAH-SHALOM, "The Lord Our Peace," reveals to us the redemptive privilege of having His peace. Accordingly, Jesus says, *"My peace I give unto you"* (John 14:27). This blessing is in the Atonement, because *"the chastisement of our peace was upon him"* (Isa. 53:5) when He *"made peace through the blood of his cross"* (Col. 1:20).

JEHOVAH-RA-AH is translated *"The LORD is my shepherd"* (Ps. 23:1). He became our Shepherd by giving *"his life for the sheep"* (John 10:11); therefore, this privilege is a redemptive privilege, purchased by the Atonement.

JEHOVAH-JIREH means "The Lord Will Provide" an offering (see Genesis 22:8), and Christ was the Offering provided for our complete redemption.

JEHOVAH-NISSI means "the Lord is our Banner" or "Victor" or "Captain." It was when, by the Cross, Christ triumphed over principalities and powers (Col. 2:15) that He provided for us, through the Atonement, the redemptive privilege of saying, *"Thanks be to God, which giveth us the victory through our Lord Jesus Christ"* (1 Cor. 15:57).

JEHOVAH-TSIDKENU is translated *"THE LORD OUR RIGHTEOUSNESS"* (Jer. 23:6). He became our righteousness by bearing our sins on the cross; therefore, our redemptive privilege of receiving *"the gift of righteousness"* (Rom. 5:17) is an Atonement blessing.

JEHOVAH-RAPHA is translated "I am the Lord your Physician" or *"I am the LORD that healeth thee"* (Exod. 15:26). This name is given to reveal to us our redemptive privilege of being healed. This privilege is purchased by the Atonement, for Isaiah, in the Redemption Chapter, declared, *"Surely he hath borne our griefs* [or sicknesses], *and carried our sorrows* [or pains]" (Isa. 53:4).

The Lord Our Physician

For the sake of the argument, I have reserved JEHOVAH-RAPHA for the last. The fact is that the very first covenant God gave after the crossing of the Red Sea—which was so distinctively typical of our redemption—was the covenant of healing; and it was at this time that God revealed Himself as our Physician, by the first redemptive and covenant name, JEHOVAH-RAPHA, *"I am the LORD that healeth thee."* This is not only a promise, but it is also *"a statute and an ordinance"* (Exod. 15:25). And so, corresponding to this ancient ordinance, we have, in the command of James 5:14–15, a positive ordinance of healing in Christ's name that is as sacred and binding upon every church today as the ordinances of the Lord's Supper and of Christian baptism:

> *Is any sick among you? let him call for the elders of the church; and let them pray over him, anointing him with oil in the name of the Lord: and the prayer of faith shall save the sick, and the Lord shall raise him up; and if he have committed sins, they shall be forgiven him.*

Since JEHOVAH-RAPHA is one of His redemptive names, sealing the covenant of healing, Christ, during His exaltation, could no more abandon His office of Healer than the offices revealed by each of His other six redemptive names. Have any of the blessings that His redemptive names reveal been withdrawn from this "better" dispensation? (See Hebrews 8:6.)

Having considered some of the types that teach healing, let us now consider the Antitype—the Atonement itself—as it is described in the great Redemption Chapter, Isaiah 53, the greatest chapter of the greatest of the prophets, in which the doctrine of the Atonement is fully stated. Since the types of the Old Testament taught healing, it is certainly unwarranted and illogical to place the Antitype on lower ground.

He Carried Our Pains

Before quoting from this chapter, may I state that the Hebrew words *choli* and *makob* in Isaiah 53:4 have been incorrectly translated as "griefs" and "sorrows."

All who have taken the time to examine the original text have found what is everywhere acknowledged, that these two words mean, respectively, "sicknesses" and "pains" everywhere else throughout the Old Testament. The word *choli* is interpreted *"sickness"* and *"disease"* in Deuteronomy 7:15; 28:61; 1 Kings 17:17; 2 Kings 1:2; 8:8; 2 Chronicles 16:12; 21:15, and other texts. The word *makob is* rendered *"pain"* in Job 33:19 and other texts. In Job 14:22, the word translated *"pain"* is *kaab,* which is the root word from which *makob* comes. Therefore, the prophet is saying, in Isaiah 53:4, *"Surely he hath borne our* [sicknesses], *and carried our* [pains]." The reader is referred to any standard Bible commentary for additional testimony on this point; however, there is no better commentary than Matthew 8:16–17.

An Inspired Commentary

That Isaiah 53:4 cannot refer to disease of the soul, and that neither of the words translated *"sickness"* and *"pain"* have any reference to spiritual matters but to bodily sickness alone, is proven by Matthew 8:16–17:

> *And* [Jesus] *cast out the spirits with his word, and healed all that were sick: that it might be fulfilled which was spoken by Esaias the prophet, saying, Himself took our infirmities, and bare our sicknesses.*

This is an inspired commentary on this fourth verse of Isaiah 53, plainly declaring that the prophet refers to bodily ailments, and therefore the word *choli,* "sickness," must be read literally in Isaiah.

The same Holy Spirit who inspired this verse quotes it in Matthew as the explanation of the universal application by Christ of His power to heal the body. To take any other view is equal to accusing the Holy Spirit of making a mistake in quoting His own prediction.

I will here quote the learned translator, Dr. Young, in his *Literal Translation of the Bible:*

> ³ *He is despised, and left of men,*
> *A man of pains [makob, Hebrew], and*
>   *acquainted with sickness [choli, Hebrew],*
> *And as one hiding the face from us,*
> *He is despised and we esteemed him not.*
> ⁴ *Surely our sicknesses [choli] he hath borne,*
> *And our pains [makob] he hath carried them,*
> *And we—we have esteemed him plagued,*
> *Smitten of God and afflicted.*
> ⁵ *And he is pierced for our transgressions*
> *Bruised for our iniquities,*
> *The chastisement of our peace is on him,*
> *And by his bruise there is healing to us.*
> ⁶ *All of us like sheep have wandered,*
> *Each to his own way we have turned,*
> *And Jehovah hath caused to meet on him*
> *The punishment of us all.*
> ¹⁰ *And Jehovah hath delighted to bruise him;*
> *He hath made him sick [choli];*
> *If his soul doth make an offering for guilt,*
> *He seeth seed—he prolongeth days.*
> ¹² *...With transgressors he was numbered,*
> *And he the sin of many hath borne,*
> *And for transgressors he intercedeth.*
>   (Isa. 53:3–6, 10, 12)

Dr. Isaac Leeser, the able translator of the Hebrew English Bible, entitled *The Twenty-Four Books of the Holy Scriptures,* renders these verses as follows:

> ³ *He was despised and shunned by men; a man*
> *of pains, and acquainted with disease....*

24

⁴ *But only our diseases did he bear himself, and
our pains he carried....*

⁵ *...and through his bruises was healing granted
to us.*

¹⁰ *But the LORD was pleased to crush him through
disease....*

Rotherham's translation of the tenth verse is,
"He laid on him sickness" (Emphasized Bible).

From You and Me to Calvary

In the fourth verse of Isaiah 53, the word *"borne"*
(*nasa*) means "to lift up, to bear away, to convey, or
to remove to a distance." It is a Levitical word, and is
applied to the scapegoat that bore away the sins of the
people. *"The goat shall bear [nasa] upon him all their
iniquities unto a land not inhabited: and he shall let go
the goat in the wilderness"* (Lev. 16:22). So Jesus bore
my sins and sicknesses away *"without ["outside," NKJV]
the camp"* (Heb. 13:13) to the cross. (See verses 11–12.)
Sin and sickness have passed from me to Calvary—salvation and health have passed from Calvary to me.

Again, in this fourth verse of the Redemption
Chapter, the Hebrew verbs for *"borne"* (*nasa*) and
"carried" (*sabal*) are both the same as are used in the
eleventh and twelfth verses for the substitutionary
bearing of sin: *"He shall bear [sabal, "carry"] their
iniquities,"* and *"He bare [nasa] the sin of many."* Both
words signify "to assume as a heavy burden," and
denote actual substitution and a complete removal of
the thing borne. When Jesus bore our sins, our sicknesses, and our pains, He bore them away, or removed
them. Both these words mean substitution, one bearing another's load.

On this point, permit me to quote from "Jesus Our Healer," a splendid tract written by the Reverend W. C. Stevens. He said,

> This prophecy presents healing as an integral part of the vicarious Atonement....Now, whatever be the sense of these two Hebrew verbs (*nasa* and *sabal*), the same sense must be applied in both cases, namely, of sin-bearing and sickness-bearing. To pervert the sense in one case would give liberty to pervert it in the other. And that the sense of the verbs as relating to sin, not only here in this prophecy, but everywhere else in the Old Testament, is strictly vicarious and expiatory, no evangelical student disputes. This prophecy, therefore, gives the same substitutionary and expiatory character to Christ's connection with sickness that is everywhere given to His assumption of our sins.

An Inspired Translation

We are accordingly held by the Spirit to the redemptive sense of Christ's bearing of sickness. This interpretation is fully sustained by Professor Delitzsch's exposition of Isaiah 53:4. Freely but faithfully does the gospel of Matthew translate this text, *"Himself took our infirmities, and bare our sicknesses"* (Matt. 8:17). The help that Jesus rendered in all kinds of bodily sickness is taken in Matthew to be a fulfillment of what in Isaiah is prophesied of the Servant of Jehovah.

The Hebrew verbs of the Isaiah 53 text, when used of sin (vv. 11–12), signify "to assume as a heavy burden and to bear away the guilt of sin as one's own"; that is, to bear sin mediatorially in order to atone for it. But in verse 4, where not sins but our sicknesses and our pains are the object, the mediatorial sense remains the same.

It is not meant that the Servant of Jehovah merely entered into the fellowship of our sufferings, but that He took upon Himself the sufferings that we had to bear and deserved to bear; and therefore He not only bore them away, but also in His own person endured them in order to discharge us from them. Now, when one takes sufferings upon himself that another had to bear, and does this not merely in fellowship with him but also in his stead, we call it substitution. Here, then, the best results of strict interpretation show that the bearing and removal of human disease is an integral part of redeeming work, a provision of the Atonement, a part of the doctrine of Christ crucified; that Jesus is the Savior of the body as well as of the spirit; and that

> He comes to make His blessings flow
> Far as the curse is found.

Someone has said,

> Bodily healing by direct divine agency becomes a boon for every believer in any period of Gospel history. It settles the question of a preacher's duty to preach it.

An Objection Answered

A Canadian writer has objected that Matthew 8:17 cannot refer to the Atonement because, since Christ had not yet been crucified, this would be "making Christ live an atoning life." This, to me, is no argument at all, since Christ is *the Lamb* [of God] *slain from the foundation of the world"* (Rev. 13:8). He not only healed disease before Calvary, but also forgave sins, and yet both of these mercies were bestowed on the ground of the Atonement still in the future.

A prominent New York clergyman has raised practically the same objection. He argues that the fact that Christ, in Matthew, is fulfilling Isaiah's prophecy by healing the sick, proves that "Jesus bore our sickness not on the cross, but when He was alive in the city of Capernaum." In answering this, I have only to ask, Did Jesus bear our *iniquities* in Capernaum or on the cross? His forgiving of sins as well as His healing of the sick were both done with respect to His coming atonement, because *"without shedding of blood is no remission"* (Heb. 9:22).

The prophecy states that *"he hath borne **our*** [sicknesses]" (Isa. 53:4). This includes all people, as well as those at Capernaum. In verses 4 and 5 of the Redemption Chapter, we see Him dying for

♦   *our* sicknesses
♦   *our* pains
♦   *our* transgressions
♦   *our* iniquities
♦   *our* peace
♦   *our* healing (for *"with his stripes we are healed"*)

We would have to misquote to exclude ourselves from any of these blessings.

The only time the word *"surely"* (v. 4) occurs in the Redemption Chapter is when it prefaces His provision for our healing. There could be no stronger statement of our complete redemption from pain and sickness by His atoning death. If Christ, as some think, is unwilling to heal as universally during His exaltation as He did during His humiliation, then He would have to break His promise in John 14:12–13:

> *Verily, verily, I say unto you, he that believeth on me, the works that I do shall he do also; and greater works than these shall he do; because I go unto my Father. And whatsoever ye shall ask in my name, that will I do, that the Father may be glorified in the Son.*

Moreover, if that were the case, He would not be *"Jesus Christ the same yesterday, and to day, and for ever"* (Heb. 13:8).

The fact of healing in the Atonement *necessitates* the continuation of His healing ministry during His exaltation, because His redeeming work embraces all who live on earth while He is with the Father. Accordingly, He gives the above promise to do the same and *"greater works"* from God's right hand in answer to our prayers. As long as the church has remained under the control of the Spirit, the same works have continued; and history reveals, as Dr. A. J. Gordon put it, "that whenever we find a revival of primitive faith and apostolic simplicity, there we find the evangelical miracles which surely characterize the apostolic age."

The apostle Paul told us, *"He hath made him to be sin for us, who knew no sin* [of his own]" (2 Cor. 5:21). Likewise, we could say, *"He hath made him to be* [sick] *for us, who knew no* [sickness of His own]." Peter wrote, *"Who his own self bare our sins in his own body on the tree"* (1 Pet. 2:24), and Isaiah declared, *"Surely he hath borne our* [sicknesses], *and carried our* [pains]" (Isa. 53:4). But, as Leeser translates it, *"Only our diseases did he bear"* (v. 4), having none of His own.

Again, in Isaiah 53:6 of Dr. Young's translation cited earlier, we read, *"And Jehovah hath caused to meet on him the punishment of us all."* One writer inquired, regarding this point, "What are the punishments of sin?" Then he said, in essence, that all will admit that sin is punished by soul condemnation, remorse, mental anxiety, and frequently by sickness, and believe these are remitted because of vicarious atonement. By what rule of Scripture or reason is the last-mentioned punishment severed from the rest? Note the prophet's words, *"Jehovah hath caused to meet on him the **punishment** of us all."* Since sickness is a part of that punishment, it is demonstrated by the immutable Word of God that sickness is included in the Atonement. The same writer then asked,

> Is it true that God will give deliverance from every penalty and consequence of sin *except one,* and that this one (sickness) must inevitably remain to the bitter end? Away with such a thought! Isaiah affirms that the *entire* punishment of us all was caused to meet on Him....He testified, "It is finished." There was nothing incomplete about the work of our mighty Jesus.

I might add to this that, were it otherwise, the prophet should have said, *"Jehovah hath caused to meet on him* [only a part of] *the punishment of us all."*

The Cross a Perfect Remedy for the Whole Man

Jesus went to the Cross in spirit, soul, and body to redeem man in spirit, soul, and body. Therefore, the Cross is the center of the plan of salvation for man—spirit, soul, and body.

Every form of sickness and disease known to man was included, and many of them are even mentioned particularly in the *"curse of the law"* (Gal. 3:13). (See, for example, Deuteronomy 28:15–68.) Now, in Galatians 3:13, we have the positive statement that *"Christ hath redeemed us from the curse of the law, being made a curse for us: for it is written, Cursed is every one that hangeth on a tree."* What plainer declaration could we have than that Christ, who was born under the law to redeem us, bore its curse, and therefore redeemed us from all sickness and disease? Here it is stated that it was on the cross that Jesus redeemed us from the law's curse. In other words, He redeemed us from the following diseases specified in Deuteronomy: *"consumption* [tuberculosis]*"* (Deut. 28:22); *"fever"* (v. 22); *"inflammation"* (v. 22); *"the botch* [boils] *of Egypt"* (v. 27); *"emerods* [tumors]*"* (v. 27); *"the scab"* (v. 27); *"the itch"* (v. 27); *"madness"* (v. 28); *"blindness"* (v. 28); *"plagues"* (v. 59); *"all the diseases of Egypt"* (v. 60); *"every sickness, and every plague, which is not written in the book of this law"* (v. 61). This would include cancer, influenza, mumps, measles, and every other modern disease. If Christ redeemed us from the curse of the law, and sickness is included in the Curse, surely He redeemed us from sickness.

Redemption Synonymous with Calvary

Redemption is synonymous with Calvary; therefore, we are redeemed from the entire Curse, body, soul, and spirit, solely through His atonement. Now, since disease is a part of the Curse, how could God justly remove this part of the Curse by healing the sick without first redeeming us from it? Again, since *"Christ hath redeemed us from the curse of the law"* (Gal. 3:13), how can God justify us and at the same time require us to remain under the law's curse, when, as the apostle Paul said, *"Ye are not under the law, but under grace"* (Rom. 6:14)? In short, why should anyone remain under the law's curse who is not under the law? To do so would be the same as putting a man in prison for life after he had been proven innocent and the court had justified him from the charge of murder.

Paul argued in Romans 3:25–26 that *"God hath set forth* [Christ] *to be a propitiation through faith in his blood,...that he might be just, and the justifier of him which believeth in Jesus."* In other words, were it not for the Atonement, God would be *unjust* in justifying the sinner; likewise, He would be unjust in healing the sick without first redeeming them from the sickness. The fact that God ever healed anyone is to me the best of proof that healing was provided by the Atonement. If healing was not provided for all in redemption, how did all in the whole multitude obtain from Christ the healing that God did not provide? *"He healed them **all"*** (Matt. 12:15, emphasis added).

An Important Question

If the body were not included in redemption, how can there be a resurrection? How can the *"corruptible...put on incorruption"* or the *"mortal...put on immortality"* (1 Cor. 15:53)? If we have not been redeemed from sickness, would we not be subject to disease in heaven, if it were possible to be resurrected irrespective of redemption? Someone has well remarked, "Man's future destiny being both spiritual and bodily, his redemption *must* be both spiritual and bodily."

Why should not the Last Adam take away all that the first Adam brought upon us?

Now let as consider a few Gospel parallels:

The Inner Man	The Outer Man
Adam, by his fall, brought sin into our souls.	Adam, by his fall, brought disease into our bodies.
Sin is therefore the work of the Devil.	Disease is therefore the work of the Devil. Jesus *"went about doing good, and healing all that were oppressed **of the devil**"* (Acts 10:38, emphasis added).
Jesus was manifested to *"destroy the works of the devil"* (1 John 3:8) in the soul.	Jesus was manifested to *"destroy the works of the devil"* (1 John 3:8) in the body.
The redemptive name Jehovah-tsidkenu reveals His redemptive provision for our souls.	The redemptive name Jehovah-rapha reveals His redemptive provision for our bodies.
On Calvary, Jesus *"bare our sins"* (1 Pet. 2:24).	On Calvary, Jesus bore our sicknesses (Isa. 53:4).
He was made *"sin for us"* (2 Cor. 5:21) when He *"bare our sins"* (1 Pet. 2:24).	He became *"a curse for us"* (Gal. 3:13) when He *"bare our sicknesses"* (Matt. 8:17).
"His own self bare our sins in his own body on the tree" (1 Pet. 2:24).	*"By whose stripes ye were healed"* (1 Pet. 2:24).

THE INNER MAN	THE OUTER MAN
"Who forgiveth all thine iniquities" (Ps. 103:3).	*"Who healeth all thy diseases"* (Ps. 103:3).
The spirit is bought with a price. *"Ye are bought with a price: therefore glorify God in your...spirit"* (1 Cor. 6:20).	The body is bought with a price. *"Ye are bought with a price: therefore glorify God in your body"* (1 Cor. 6:20).
Is remaining in sin the way to glorify God in your spirit?	Is remaining in sin the way to glorify God in your body?
Since He *"bare **our** sins"* (1 Pet. 2:24, emphasis added), how many *must* it be God's will to save, when they come to Him? *"Whosoever believeth"* (John 3:16).	Since He *"bare **our** sicknesses"* (Matt. 8:17, emphasis added), how many *must* it be God's will to heal, when they come to Him? *"He healed them all"* (Matt. 12:15).
"As God *'made him to be sin for us, who knew no sin'* (2 Cor. 5:21),	...so God made Him to be sick for us who knew no sickness." —Rev. A. J. Gordon
"Since our Substitute bore our sins, did He not do so that we might not bare them?" —Rev. A. J. Gordon	"Since our Substitute bore our sicknesses, did He not do so that we might not bare them?" —Rev. A. J. Gordon
"Christ bore our sins that we might be delivered from them. Not SYMPATHY—a suffering *with,* but SUBSTITUTION—a suffering *for.*" —Rev. A. J. Gordon	"Christ bore our sicknesses that we might be delivered from them. Not SYMPATHY—a suffering *with,* but SUBSTITUTION—a suffering *for.*" —Rev. A. J. Gordon

The Inner Man	The Outer Man
"If the fact that Jesus *'bare our sins in his own body on the tree'* (1 Pet. 2:24) be a valid reason why we should all trust Him now for the forgiveness of our sins,	...why is not the fact that He *'bare our sicknesses'* (Matt. 8:17), an equally valid reason why we should all trust Him now to heal our bodies?" —Writer unknown
Faith for salvation *"cometh by hearing"* (Rom. 10:17) the Gospel—He *"bare our sins"* (1 Pet. 2:24).	Faith for healing *"cometh by hearing"* (Rom. 10:17) —He *"bare our sicknesses"* (Matt. 8:17).
Therefore, *"preach the gospel* [that He bore our sins] *to every creature"* (Mark 16:15),	...and *"the gospel* [that He bore our sicknesses] *to every creature"* (Mark 16:15).
Christ's promise for the soul (*"shall be saved"*) is in the Great Commission (Mark 16:16).	Christ's promise for the body (*"shall recover"*) is in the Great Commission (Mark 16:18).
In connection with the ordinance of baptism, the Bible teaches that *"he that believeth and is baptized shall be saved"* (Mark 16:16).	In connection with the ordinance of anointing with oil, the Bible teaches that he who believes and is anointed will be healed (James 5:14–15).
We are commanded to baptize in Christ's name.	We are commanded to anoint *"in the name of the Lord"* (James 5:14).
In the Lord's Supper, the wine is taken *"in remembrance"* of His death for our souls (1 Cor. 11:25).	In the Lord's Supper, the bread is eaten *"in remembrance"* of His death for our bodies (1 Cor. 11:23–24).

THE INNER MAN	THE OUTER MAN
The sinner is to repent before believing the Gospel *"unto righteousness"* (Rom. 10:10).	James 5:16 says, *"Confess your faults [sins] one to another,...that ye may be healed."*
Water baptism stands for total surrender and obedience.	Anointing with oil is the symbol and sign of consecration.
The sinner must accept God's promise as true before he can feel the joy of salvation.	The sick one must accept God's promise as true before he can feel well.
"As many as received him...were born...of God" (John 1:12–13, emphasis added).	*"As many as touched him were made whole"* (Mark 6:56, emphasis added).

A Testimony of Healing

I will now cite one out of many hundreds of cases of sickness and affliction that have been healed while the sufferers listened to preaching on the subject of healing in the Atonement. Their healing came through their own faith before having an opportunity of being anointed.

When only an eight-year-old child, Mrs. Clara Rupert of Lima, Ohio, had such a severe case of whooping cough that she ruptured the muscles of one eye, leaving it entirely blind and so dead that during all the years that followed she could rub her finger on the bare eyeball without pain. She said that on windy days, when particles would blow into the eye, it caused her no suffering.

While listening to a sermon on the Atonement during our revival in Lima, Ohio, she said in her heart, "If that is true, and it is because the Bible says so, then I am just as sure of receiving sight in my blind eye tonight when I go to the altar as I was sure of salvation when I went to the Methodist altar several years ago and was saved." Accordingly, with this logical reasoning, she came to the altar, and while we were praying with others, she asked God to heal her. Before we had a chance to anoint her, she was on her feet weeping, and she walked back and threw her arms around her father's neck, the audience wondering why she had left the altar without being anointed. Her father asked, "What is the matter, daughter?" and she replied, "My eye!" He said, "Why, is it paining you?" She said, "No, I can see perfectly!"

A few months later, while we were holding a revival in St. Paul, Minnesota, we met this woman and her husband, who were there attending the Bible school, preparing for work for the Master.

Her husband wanted to preach the Gospel of Christ, who had so graciously healed his wife.

Almost daily in our revivals, testimonies are given by those who have been healed while sitting in their seats listening to the Gospel.

What Renowned Bible Teachers Have to Say

These views on healing in the Atonement are not new and unique only to myself. Many of the most godly and able teachers of the church have seen and taught them. In addition to those teachers already quoted, I will add a few words from Dr. R. A. Torrey and others.

Dr. Torrey, in his book discussing divine healing, declared,

The atoning death of Jesus Christ secured for us not only physical healing, but the resurrection and perfecting and glorifying of our bodies....The Gospel of Christ has salvation for the body as well as for the soul....Just as one gets the firstfruits of his spiritual salvation in the life that now is, so we get the firstfruits of our physical salvation in the life that now is....Individual believers, whether elders or not, have the privilege and the duty to *"pray one for another"* (James 5:16) in case of sickness with the expectation that God will hear and heal.

Dr. R. E. Stanton, a former moderator of the General Assembly of the Presbyterian Church, gave the following in his *Gospel Parallelisms:*

It is my aim to show that the atonement of Christ lays the foundation equally for deliverance from sin and for deliverance from disease. That complete provision has been made for both; that in the exercise of faith under the conditions prescribed, we have the same reason to believe that the body may be delivered from sickness as we have that the soul shall be delivered from sin; in short, that both branches of the deliverance stand on the same ground, and that it is necessary to include both in any true conception of what the Gospel offers to mankind. The atoning sacrifice of Christ covers the physical as well as the spiritual needs of the race....Healing of the body is not, therefore, a "side issue," as some represent it. It is no more this than the healing of the soul is a "side issue." They are both but parts of the same Gospel, based equally upon the same great Atonement.

The Episcopal Church on Divine Healing

In the report of the commission on spiritual healing appointed by the Episcopal Church, sponsored by Bishop Reese, who for many years has practiced the healing ministry, and who was Chairman of the commission, is the following statement:

> The healing of the body is an essential element of the Gospel, and must be preached and practiced....God wills our health, that the church, the "body of Christ," has the same commission and the same power as "the Head," that we churchmen, with this true conception of God as Creative Love, must now give a sinning and suffering world this full Gospel of salvation from sin and its inevitable consequences.

These conclusions were arrived at by this scholarly commission after three years of study and research.

Bishop Charles H. Brent of the Episcopal Church, who, as Head of all Chaplains in France, led the religious life of our armies overseas, affirmed:

> He who waives away the healing power of Christ as belonging only to the New Testament times is not preaching the whole Gospel. God was, and is, the Savior of the body as well as the soul.

James Moore Hickson pleaded,

> A living church is one in which the living Christ lives and walks, doing through its members what He did in the days of His flesh. It must, therefore, be a *healing* church as well as a

39

soul-saving church....Spiritual healing is sacramental. It is the extension through the members of His mystical body of His own incarnate life.

The late able writers Dr. A. B. Simpson, Andrew Murray, A. T. Pierson, Dr. A. J. Gordon, and many present writers whom we might quote, have been teachers of healing in the Atonement. One writer has said, "On the cross of Calvary, Jesus has nailed the proclamation, 'Deliver from going down to the pit (grave), for I have found an Atonement.'" (See Job 33:24.)

Isaiah begins the Redemption Chapter with the question, *"Who hath believed our report? and to whom is the arm of the LORD revealed?"* (Isa. 53:1). And the report follows that He bore our sins and sicknesses (vv. 4–5). The answer to the question is that only those who have heard the report can have believed it, because *"faith cometh by hearing"* (Rom. 10:17). Since Jesus died to save and to heal, it is surely worth reporting.

The purpose of this chapter is to prove that healing is provided by the Atonement and is therefore a part of the Gospel that Christ commanded to be preached

- to *"all the world"* (Mark 16:15)
- to *"all nations"* (Matt. 28:19)
- to *"every creature"* (Mark 16:15)
- with *"all power"* (Matt. 28:18)
- throughout *"alway* [all the days, Greek], *even unto the end of the* [present] *world* [age]" (Matt. 28:20)

Two

✦

Is Healing for All?

Two

✦

Is Healing for All?

I s it still the will of God, as in the past, to heal all who have need of healing (Luke 9:11), and to fulfill the number of their days (Exod. 23:26)? The greatest barrier to the faith of many seeking bodily healing in our day is the uncertainty in their minds as to its being the will of God to heal *all*. Nearly everyone knows that God does heal *some,* but there is much in modern theology that keeps people from knowing what the Bible clearly teaches—that healing is provided for all. It is impossible to boldly claim by faith a blessing that we are not sure God offers, because the power of God can be claimed only where the will of God is known.

It would be next to impossible to get a sinner to "[believe] *unto righteousness"* (Rom. 10:10) before you had fully convinced him that it was God's will to save him.

Faith begins where the will of God is known. If it is God's will to heal only some of those who need healing, then none have any basis for faith, unless they have a special revelation that they are among the favored ones. Faith must rest on the will of God alone, not on our desires or wishes. Appropriating faith is not believing that God *can* but that God *will.* Because of not knowing it to be a redemptive privilege for all, most people in our day, when seeking healing, add to their petition, "If it is Your will."

A Corrected Theology

Among all those who sought healing from Christ during His earthly ministry, we read of only one who had this kind of theology. This was the leper, who said, *"Lord, if thou wilt, thou canst make me clean"* (Matt. 8:2). The first thing Christ did was to correct his theology by saying, *"I will; be thou clean"* (v. 3). Christ's *"I will"* cancelled his *"if,"* adding to the man's faith that Christ *could* heal him, the faith that He *would*.

The theology of this leper, before Christ enlightened him, is almost universal today, because this part of the Gospel is so seldom and so fragmentarily preached.

We see, from almost every conceivable angle throughout the Scriptures, that there is no doctrine more clearly taught than that it is God's will to heal all who have need of healing, and that they may fulfill the number of their days, according to His promise (Exod. 23:26). Of course, we mean all who are properly taught and who meet the conditions prescribed in the Word. Now, I hear someone say, "If healing is for all, then we will never die." Why not? Divine healing goes no further than the promise of God. He does not promise that we will never physically die, but He says, *"I will take sickness away from the midst of thee....The number of thy days I will fulfil"* (vv. 25–26). Consider the following texts:

> *The days of our years are threescore years and ten* [seventy]; *and if by reason of strength they be fourscore years* [eighty].   *(Ps. 90:10)*

Take me not away in the midst of my days.
                                    (Ps. 102:24)

Why shouldest thou die before thy time?
                                    (Eccl. 7:17)

Then someone may ask, Well, how is a man going to die?

Thou takest away their breath, they die, and return to their dust.   *(Ps. 104:29)*

The Reverend P. Gavin Duffy wrote on this point,

He has allotted to man a certain span of life, and His will is that that life shall be lived out. I want you to recall that all those He called back from the dead were *young people* who had not lived out their fullness of years; and in that very fact we may well see His protest against premature death....Of course, we must not expect that the old shall be physically young, but if the allotted span has not been spent, we have a right to claim God's gift of health; and, even though it be past, if it be His will that we should continue here for a time longer, it is equally His will that we should do so in good health.

Death comes, and then we blame our God,
    And weakly say, "Thy will be done";
But never underneath the sod
    Has God imprisoned any one.
God does not send disease, or crime,
    Or carelessness, or fighting clans;
And when we die before our time,
    The fault is man's.

He is a God of life, not death;
   He is one God that gives us birth;
He has not shortened by a breath
   The life of any on the earth;
And He would have us dwell within
   The world our full allotted years.
So blame not God—for our own sin
   Makes our own tears.
               —Douglas Malloch

Read the Will and Know

If we want to know what is in a will, let us read the will. If we want to know God's will on any subject, let us read His will. Suppose a lady said, "My husband, who was very rich, has passed away; now, I wish I knew whether he left me anything in his will." I would say to her, "Why don't you read the will and see?" The word *testament,* legally speaking, means a person's will. The Bible contains God's last will and testament, in which He bequeaths to us all the blessings of redemption; and since it is His "*last* will and testament," anything later is a forgery. A man never writes a new will after he is dead. If healing is in God's will for us, then to say that the age of miracles is past is virtually saying what is the opposite of the truth, that a will is no good after the death of the testator. Jesus is not only the Testator who died, but He was resurrected, and He is also the Mediator of the will (Heb. 8:6). He is our lawyer, so to speak, and He will not cheat us out of the will, as some earthly lawyers do. He is our Representative at *"the right hand of God"* (Mark 16:19).

For the answer to the question under consideration, let us look away from modern tradition and go to the Word of God, which is a revelation of His will.

In the fifteenth chapter of Exodus, just after the passage about the crossing of the Red Sea, which typified our redemption and was *"written for our admonition"* (1 Cor. 10:11), God gave His first promise to heal (Exod. 15:26). This promise was for *all*. God named the conditions, the conditions were met, and we read, in Psalm 105:37, that *"he brought them forth also with silver and gold: and there was not one feeble person among their tribes."* It was here that God gave the covenant of healing, revealed by and sealed with His first covenant and redemptive name, Jehovah-rapha, translated, *"I am the Lord that healeth thee"* (Exod. 15:26). This is God's Word, *"settled in heaven"* (Ps. 119:89), a never changing fact concerning God.

Who Is Authorized to Change God's Will?

To say that this privilege of health is not for God's people today is to change God's "I *am* Jehovah-rapha" to "I *was* Jehovah-rapha." Who has the authority to change God's redemptive names? Instead of abandoning His office as Healer, He is *"Jesus Christ the same yesterday, and to day, and for ever"* (Heb. 13:8) under this first covenant name as well as under the other six. The blessings revealed by His redemptive names, as we have seen in the preceding chapter, were provided by the Atonement, when He *"taste[d] death for every man"* (Heb. 2:9, emphasis added), and therefore cannot be confined to Israel. This fifteenth chapter of Exodus shows us that, at least in that age of the world, 3,500 years ago, God did not leave the people in doubt concerning His willingness to heal *all*.

A Nation without One Feeble Person

This universal state of health in the nation of Israel continued as long as God's conditions were met. Then, twenty years later, because of sin, a plague destroyed 14,700 people. When they again met the conditions, the plague was stopped, and He was still JEHOVAH-RAPHA, the Healer, not to some, but to all. (See Numbers 16:46–50.) It would not be true that the plague was stopped if it remained on even one of them. This state of health again remained uninterrupted until nineteen years later, when the people, not satisfied with God's way for them, chosen in love and mercy, spoke against God and against Moses, and they were cursed with the fiery serpents. (See Numbers 21:4–9.) When they again met God's conditions, by confessing their sins (v. 7), His word through Moses to them was, *"It shall come to pass, that **every one** that is bitten, when he looketh upon it* [the bronze serpent—the type of Calvary], *shall live"* (v. 8, emphasis added). So, again, at this time, the Scriptures show us that it was still God's will to heal not some, but all. *Every one* who was bitten lived by looking at the bronze serpent, which was a typical foreshadowing of Christ's coming sacrifice upon Calvary in our behalf.

The psalmist David, in his time, understood healing to be a universal privilege. In Psalm 86, he said, *"For thou, Lord, art good,…plenteous in mercy unto **all** them that call upon thee"* (v. 5, emphasis added). We will see, in the next chapter, that healing was one of the most prominent mercies throughout the Scriptures, and that the sick, in the New Testament, asked for "mercy" when seeking healing from Christ—for God's mercy covers man's physical, as well as spiritual, nature. Therefore, Jesus, according to the Old

Testament promise, showed that He was *"plenteous in mercy"* by healing not *some,* but *all* who came to Him. (See, for example, Matthew 8:16; 9:35; 12:15; Mark 6:56; Luke 4:40; 6:19; 9:11.)

Also, in Psalm 103, we see that David believed that the mercy of healing was as universal a privilege as the mercy of forgiveness. He called upon his soul to bless God, *"Who forgiveth **all** thine iniquities; who healeth **all** thy diseases"* (v. 3, emphasis added). *"Who healeth **all**"* is as permanent as *"Who forgiveth **all**,"* for the identical language is used with reference to both mercies.

In Psalm 91, God says concerning the one *"that dwelleth in the secret place of the most High"* (v. 1), *"With long life will I satisfy him"* (v. 16). Is the privilege of dwelling in the *"secret place"* only for a few or for all? If it is for all, then God's promise to *all* is, *"With long life will I satisfy him."* God would have to break this promise to be unwilling to heal His obedient children in middle life. If dwelling in the secret place was possible in a darker age of the world, surely it is possible in this better age of grace, during which *"God is able to make all grace abound"* (2 Cor. 9:8) toward each of His children. The holy prophets of the Old Testament *"prophesied of the grace that should come unto* [us]" (1 Pet. 1:10).

Calvary Heals All Men's Ills

We have seen, in the great Redemption Chapter, Isaiah 53, that it is *our* sicknesses, as well as *our* sins, that Jesus bore, making one privilege as universal as the other. What Jesus did for individuals who came to Him for blessings was for *them,* but what He did on Calvary was for *all.*

It is clear, in all of these instances cited from the Old Testament, that it was God's will to heal all who met the conditions. Whenever forgiveness was offered, healing was also offered. Let those who teach the people that God's will in the matter of healing is not the same today answer the question, Why would God withdraw this Old Testament mercy from this better dispensation? Is it not to be expected that He who has reserved better things for us (see 1 Peter 1:4) and who is the same yesterday, today, and forever (Heb. 13:8) should continue these same mercies throughout this better dispensation? Let us now look in the New Testament and see.

Christ Is the Expression of God's Will

There is no better way of ascertaining the proper answer to the question before us than by reading the Gospels, which record the teachings and the works of Christ. He was the expression of the Father's will. His life was both a revelation and a manifestation of the unchanging love and will of God. He literally acted out the will of God for Adam's race. He said, *"I came down from heaven, not to do mine own will, but the will of him that sent me"* (John 6:38), and *"The Father that dwelleth in me, he doeth the works"* (John 14:10). He also said, *"He that hath seen me hath seen the Father"* (v. 9); therefore, when He healed the multitudes who thronged Him day after day, we see the Father revealing His will. When He *"laid his hands on **every one** of them, and healed them"* (Luke 4:40, emphasis added), He was doing and revealing the will of God for *our* bodies.

Perhaps no one would be more conservative than the scholars of the Episcopal Church, and yet the commission appointed to study the subject of spiritual healing and report back to the Church, after three years of study and research in both the Bible and history, said in its report, "The healing of the sick by Jesus was done as a revelation of God's will for man." Because the members of the commission discovered that His will is fully revealed, the report further says, "No longer can the Church pray for the sick with the *faith-destroying,* qualifying phrase 'If it be Thy will.'"

The message everywhere taught in the Gospels is one of complete healing for soul and body for all who come to Him. Many today say, "I believe in healing, but I do not believe it is for everyone." If it is not, how can we pray the prayer of faith for any, or even for one whom it is God's will to heal, until we have a revelation by the Spirit that we are praying for the right one? If it is not God's will to heal all, then no one can ascertain the will of God for himself from the Bible. Are we to understand from these teachers that we must close our Bibles and get our revelation directly from the Spirit before we can pray for the sick, because the will of God cannot be ascertained from the Scriptures?

This would be virtually teaching that all divine activity along the lines of healing would have to be governed by the direct revelation of the Spirit, instead of by the Scriptures. How are the sick to be healed if there is no Gospel ("good news") of healing to proclaim to them as a basis for their faith? Or, since faith is expecting God to keep His promise, how can there be faith for healing if there is no promise in the Bible that the sick person can apply to himself? The Scriptures tell us how God heals the sick: *"He sent his word, and healed them, and delivered them from their destructions* [graves]" (Ps. 107:20). *"The **word** of God...effectually worketh also in* [those] *that believe"* (1 Thess. 2:13, emphasis added), and is *"health to all their flesh"* (Prov. 4:22).

Faith Rests on More than Mere Ability

If a millionaire were to appear before an audience of a thousand people, with the announcement that he was *able* to give each one a thousand dollars, this would be no basis for any to have faith for a thousand dollars, because faith cannot rest on ability. If he should go further and say, "I will give fifty of you a thousand dollars each," even then there is no basis for anyone in the audience to have faith for the thousand dollars. Were you to ask one of them if he or she were "fully assured" of receiving a thousand dollars from the millionaire, the answer would be, "I need the money, and hope I am among the lucky ones, but I cannot be sure." But if the millionaire were to say, "It is my will to give everyone a thousand dollars each," then everyone in the audience would have a ground for faith, and would undoubtedly say to the rich man, "Thank you! I'll take my money."

Now, supposing God were a *"respecter of persons* ["exhibiting partiality," Greek]" (Acts 10:34), and that it was His will to heal only some of those who need healing, let us take a glance through the Gospels, and see how the friends of the sick decided which of the sick to bring to Him for healing. *"Now when the sun was setting, all they that had any sick with divers diseases brought them unto him; and he laid his hands on every one of them, and healed them"* (Luke 4:40). Here the "unlucky" ones, if there were any, were brought, and all of them were healed the same as the others.

Surely, this was God doing and revealing His own will.

If you had been there and were sick, you would have been brought, and would have been healed with the rest, because *all* were brought, and *all* were healed. Matthew, in his record of this instance, told why Jesus made no exceptions: *"He...healed all that were sick: that it might be fulfilled which was spoken by Esaias the prophet, saying, Himself took our infirmities, and bare our sicknesses"* (Matt. 8:16–17). The word *"our"* means everybody, in the sacrifice of Calvary, and it therefore requires the healing of all to fulfill the prophecy. Not only on this occasion, but on every occasion since, down until today, He heals the sick so *"that it might be fulfilled which was spoken by Esaias the prophet, saying, Himself took our infirmities, and bare our sicknesses."*

Let the sick go through the Gospels and note the *all*s and the *every*s, and they will see that the redemptive blessing of healing was for all, and that no one ever appealed in vain to Jesus for healing. There never was a multitude large enough to have in it even one whom Jesus wanted to remain sick, and would not heal.

Jesus Healed Everything and Everyone

*And Jesus went about all Galilee, teaching ...and preaching the gospel...and healing **all manner** of sickness and **all manner** of disease among the people. And his fame went throughout all Syria: and they brought unto him all sick people that were taken with divers diseases and torments, and those which were possessed with devils, and those which were lunatic, and those*

that had the palsy; and he healed them ["all,"
MOFFATT]. *And there followed him great multitudes of people from Galilee, and from Decapolis, and from Jerusalem, and from Judaea, and
from beyond Jordan.*
(Matt. 4:23–25, emphasis added)

*And Jesus went about all the cities and villages,
teaching...and preaching the gospel...and healing every sickness and every disease among the
people. But when he saw the multitudes, he was
moved with compassion on them....And when
he had called unto him his twelve disciples, he
gave them power against unclean spirits, to cast
them out, and to heal all manner of sickness and
all manner of disease.*   *(Matt. 9:35–36; 10:1)*

Note that it was the multitudes coming for healing that necessitated the thrusting forth of new laborers into His harvest to preach and to heal. It was
not long until seventy more were needed and were
sent forth to heal as well as to preach. Let us look at
several more Scriptures that show that Jesus healed
everyone who came to Him for healing:

*Jesus...withdrew himself from thence: and great
multitudes followed him, and he healed them
all.*   *(Matt. 12:15)*

*And Jesus went forth, and saw a great multi-
tude, and was moved with compassion toward
them, and he healed their sick.*   *(Matt. 14:14)*

And when [Jesus and His disciples] *were gone
over, they came into the land of Gennesaret. And
when the men of that place had knowledge of
him, they sent out into all that country round*

*about, and brought unto him all that were dis-
eased; and besought him that they might only
touch the hem of his garment: and as many as
touched were made perfectly whole.*
(Matt. 14:34–36)

*A great multitude of people out of all Judaea and
Jerusalem, and from the sea coast of Tyre and
Sidon, which came to hear him, and to be healed
of their diseases; and they that were vexed with
unclean spirits: and they were healed. And the
whole multitude sought to touch him: for there
went virtue out of him, and healed them all.*
(Luke 6:17–19)

We see throughout the Gospels that, in bringing
the sick to Christ for healing, it was repeatedly stated
that *all* the sick were brought, which included all the
"unlucky" ones whom it was supposedly not God's will
to heal, if there were any. If, according to modern tradition, it is God's will for the sick to patiently remain
so for His glory, is it not strange that there should
not be even one of this type of person in all these multitudes who were brought to Christ for healing? By
healing the epileptic (Mark 9:14–29), Jesus proved it
to be the Father's will to heal even this one whom the
disciples, divinely commissioned to cast out demons,
failed to deliver. We see by this passage that it would
have been wrong to call into question God's willingness to heal, and to teach it, because of this failure
on the part of the disciples. Jesus, by healing him,
showed them that the failure to heal proved nothing
but unbelief. Peter, after three years of constant asso-
ciation with the Lord, described His earthly ministry
in this one brief statement: *"God anointed Jesus of
Nazareth with the Holy Ghost and with power: who*

went about doing good, and healing all that were oppressed of the devil; for God was with him" (Acts 10:38).

So, in all the above Scriptures, and in many others that show He healed all the sick, we have the will of God revealed for our bodies, and the answer to the question, Is healing for all?

Three

✦

Christ's Continuing Ministry of Healing

Three

✦

Christ's Continuing Ministry of Healing

Many in our day have been taught that Christ performed miracles of healing just to show His power and to prove His deity. This may be true, but it is far from being all the truth. He would not have had to heal *all* to show His power; a few outstanding cases would have proven this. But the Scriptures show that He healed because of His compassion and to fulfill prophecy. Others teach that He healed the sick to make Himself known, but in Matthew 12:15–16, we read, *"Great multitudes followed him, and he healed them all; and charged them that they should **not make him known**"* (emphasis added).

Some who have to admit that Jesus healed all who came to Him hold that Isaiah's prophecy concerning His bearing of our sicknesses refers only to His earthly ministry, that this universal manifestation of His compassion was special and not a revelation of the unchanging will of God. But the Bible clearly teaches that He only *"began both to do and teach"* (Acts 1:1) what was not only to be continued, but also augmented, after His ascension.

After Christ, for three years, had healed all who came to Him, He said, *"It is expedient* [profitable] *for you that I go away"* (John 16:7). How could this be true if His going away would modify His ministry to the afflicted?

Anticipating the unbelief with which this wonderful promise would be regarded, He prefaced His promise to continue the same and *"greater works"* in answer to our prayers after His exaltation, with the words *"verily, verily"*:

> *Verily, verily, I say unto you, he that believeth on me, the works that I do shall he do also; and greater works than these shall he do; because I go unto my Father. And* [how are we to do them?] *whatsoever ye shall ask in my name, that will **I** do, that the Father may be glorified in the Son.*   *(John 14:12–13, emphasis added)*

In other words, we are to do them by asking *Him* to do them.

He did not say "less works," but *"the works"* and *"greater works."*

To me, this promise from the lips of Christ is a complete answer to all opposers and to all their books and articles against divine healing.

"It is written" was Christ's policy when resisting the Devil. (See, for example, Matthew 4:4.)

William Jennings Bryan well asked, "Since Christ said 'It is written,' and the devil said 'It is written,' why can't the preacher say 'It is written?'"

The Wisdom of the Early Church

The early church took Christ at His word and prayed unitedly for signs and wonders of healing, until *"the place was shaken where they were assembled together"* (Acts 4:31); and then

> *they brought forth the sick into the streets, and*
> *laid them on beds and couches....There came*
> *also a multitude out of the cities round about*
> *unto Jerusalem, bringing sick folks, and them*
> *which were vexed with unclean spirits: and they*
> *were healed every one.*   *(Acts 5:15–16)*

The Gospels describe *"all that Jesus **began** both to do and teach"* (Acts 1:1, emphasis added). In this incident in the book of Acts, Jesus was continuing His ministry from the right hand of God through His *"body, the church"* (Col. 1:18), according to His promise. Some say, "Oh, that was only in the beginning of the Acts of the Apostles, for the purpose of confirming their word regarding Christ's resurrection."

Let us, then, turn to the *last* chapter of Acts, and read how, thirty years later, after Paul, on the island of Melita, had healed the father of Publius, *"all the other sick people in the island came and were cured"* (Acts 28:9 WEYMOUTH).

So we see again, even at this time, in the very last chapter of the Acts of the Holy Spirit, which is the only unfinished book of the New Testament, it was still the will of God to heal not some, but all.

The Acts of the Holy Spirit

The Holy Spirit, whom Christ sent as His Successor and Executive, took possession of the church, which is the body of Christ, and showed the same healing power after Pentecost that Christ had displayed before, and vast multitudes were healed. In Acts, as well as the Gospels, we never read of anyone asking for healing and being denied. Men have named this book "The Acts of the Apostles." A better and a truer

name for this book would be "The Acts of the Holy
Spirit," because it records the acts of the Holy Spirit
through not only the apostles, but also other believers. Philip and Stephen, who were not apostles, were
as gloriously used as Peter and John. The Holy Spirit
came to execute for us all the blessings purchased
by Christ's redemption, and pledged by the seven
redemptive names. He has never lost any of His inter-
est in the work He came to do. If you wish to know how
He wants to act today, read how He has acted. The
book of Acts shows us how He wants to act throughout *"alway* [all the days, Greek], *even unto the end of
the world* [age]*"* (Matt. 28:20).

It was the Holy Spirit who worked all the miracles
of healing at the hands of Christ. Jesus never under-
took a miracle until, in answer to His prayer, the Holy
Spirit, the Miracle Worker, came upon Him; and then,
in full reliance upon the Spirit, He cast out demons
and healed the sick. The miracles of Christ were all
done by the Spirit in advance of the Spirit's own dispensation, or before He had yet entered officially into
office. Why would the Holy Spirit, who healed all the
sick before His dispensation began, do less after He
entered office? Did the Miracle Worker enter office to
do away with miracles during His own dispensation?

Is the teaching and the practice of the church in
the matter of healing in this Laodicean (lukewarm;
see Revelation 3:14–18) period of her history a truer
expression of the will of God than the teaching and
practice of the early church while under the full sway
of the Spirit? Decidedly not! I do not hesitate to say
that modern theology has robbed the Holy Spirit of a
part of His ministry.

Now, in summing up so far, we have seen a revelation from many angles of Christ's merciful attitude

toward our sicknesses and infirmities since His exaltation at the right hand of God.

Christ's Present Attitude toward Sickness and Disease

We will now deal not with the past, but with Christ's present attitude toward sickness and disease.

First, Christ's present attitude is fully revealed by His redemptive name JEHOVAH-RAPHA. His redemptive names cannot change. All will admit that His other six redemptive names are a revelation of His present attitude in the matter of bestowing the blessing that each name was given to reveal. By what logic, then, can we suppose that He has abandoned His office as Healer, revealed by the name JEHOVAH-RAPHA?

Second, His present attitude is again fully revealed by His own definite promise to continue and augment His healing ministry in answer to the prayers of believers while He is at the right hand of God.

> *Verily, verily, I say unto you, He that believeth on me, the works that I do shall he do also; and greater works than these shall he do; because I go unto my Father. And whatsoever ye shall ask in my name, that will I do, that the Father may be glorified in the Son.* (John 14:12–13)

Third, His present attitude is revealed by His own fulfillment of the above promise, recorded in the book of Acts. Even in the very last chapter, thirty years after His ascension, we read, *"All the other sick people in the island came and were cured"* (Acts 28:9 WEYMOUTH).

Fourth, His present attitude is revealed by the fact that healing is a part of the Gospel that Christ commanded to be preached

- to *"all the world"* (Mark 16:15)
- to *"all nations"* (Matt. 28:19)
- to *"every creature"* (Mark 16:15)
- throughout *"alway* [all the days, Greek], *even unto the end of the* [present] *world* [age]" (Matt. 28:20)

This commission is followed by the promise, *"They shall lay hands on the sick, and they shall recover"* (Mark 16:18).

Fifth, His present attitude is revealed by the fact that His substitutionary work on Calvary was not only for His followers at the time that He was on the earth, but also in behalf of all those who live on earth during His exaltation at the right hand of the Father. We saw in the first chapter that, as in Leviticus it is recorded that all disease was healed on the ground of atonement, so Matthew tells us that the Atonement was Christ's reason for making no exceptions in healing the sick who came to Him (Matt. 8:16–17).

Sixth, His present attitude is revealed by the plain command to *"any sick"* in the church, while He is with the Father, to ask for anointing and prayer with the promise that *"the Lord shall raise him up"* (James 5:14–15). Does He mean we should pray with faith or without it? How can we pray *"the prayer of faith"* (v. 15) unless it is His will to heal, or does He command us to pray for something He will not do? Right in this passage, even laymen are commanded to *"confess* [their] *faults one to another, and pray one for another"* for healing (v. 16), with the same earnestness with which Elijah prayed for rain. (See verses 16–18.)

Would God command us to thus entreat Him for what it is not His will to do? Certainly not!

Seventh, His present attitude is revealed by the fact that it was after His exaltation that He *"set* [established]...*in the church...teachers...miracles...gifts of healings,"* and so forth (1 Cor. 12:28), for the continuance of *"the* [same] *works"* and *"greater works"* (John 14:12) that He promised He would continue from God's right hand. History records the manifestation of these miraculous gifts from the days of the apostles down to the present time.

The Unchangeable Compassion of Jesus

Eighth, His present attitude toward our sicknesses is wonderfully revealed by the fact that since His exaltation, His compassion has neither been withdrawn nor modified.

In the next chapter, on the subject of the Lord's compassion, we will see that during the earthly ministry of our Lord, He was always *"moved with compassion"* (see, for example, Matthew 14:14; Mark 1:41), and healed all *"that had need of healing"* (Luke 9:11). The same Greek word in the New Testament that is translated "mercy" is also repeatedly translated "compassion," for they are the same. When two blind men asked for mercy, Jesus was moved with compassion, and He healed them. (See Matthew 20:29–34.)

Since bodily healing, in the New Testament, is always a mercy (it was mercy, or compassion, that moved Him to heal all who came to Him), is not the promise still true that He is *"plenteous in mercy unto **all** them that call upon* [Him]" (Ps. 86:5, emphasis added)?

Does not this glorious Gospel dispensation offer as much mercy and compassion to its sufferers as did the darker dispensation? The Reverend Kenneth Mackenzie, a noted teacher and writer of the Episcopal Church, asked, regarding this point,

Could the loving heart of the Son of God, who had compassion upon the sick, and healed all who had need of healing, cease to regard the sufferings of His own when He had become exalted at the right hand of the Father?

An Absurd Feature of Modern Theology

Is it not strange that anyone in this better age of grace should take a position that would be synonymous with saying that the manifestation of Christ's compassion to the afflicted has been withdrawn, or even modified, since His glorification? If God is not as willing to show the mercy of healing to His *worshippers* as He is to show the mercy of forgiveness to His *enemies,* then He is more willing to show mercy to the Devil's children than to His own. The Scriptures deny this by saying, *"The mercy* [compassion] *of the LORD is from everlasting to everlasting* [not upon the sinner alone, but] *upon them that fear him"* (Ps. 103:17); for He loves His own sick and suffering child even more than He loves the sinner. Thank God, His mercy (compassion) is unto all generations. (See Luke 1:50.)

Ninth, His present attitude is revealed by the fact that, in the Old Testament Year of Jubilee, which Jesus applied to the Gospel era (see Luke 4:17–19), it was *"every man"* who was told to return to his possession (Lev. 35:10). In the Year of Jubilee, the blessings were for *"every man"*; in the same way, in the Gospel era, the blessings are for *"every creature"* (Mark 16:15). This truth is more fully developed in the first chapter of this book.

Tenth, His present attitude is also revealed by the fact that "[He] *hath redeemed us* [all of us] *from the curse of the law"* (Gal. 3:13). We saw in chapter one that this Curse includes all the diseases known to history. How can God justify us and at the same time require us to remain under the Curse from which He redeemed us?

The Guarantee of Complete Redemption

Eleventh, His present attitude is revealed by the fact that the Holy Spirit and His work in us is *"the earnest* [*"guarantee,"* NKJV] *of our inheritance until the redemption of the purchased possession"* (Eph. 1:14). I have already pointed out that because our eternal destiny is both spiritual and physical, our redemption also *must* be both spiritual and physical. Therefore, we cannot receive our full inheritance until the coming Day of Redemption; but, thank God, by being filled with the Spirit, we now have *"the earnest"* of it. Paul told us that we *"have the firstfruits of the Spirit"* (Rom. 8:23, emphasis added), and these are manifested both spiritually and physically. The *"first-fruits of the Spirit"* include the earnest of immortality, which is a foretaste of the resurrection.

Since our bodies are members of Christ, His glorified bodily life is as truly linked with our bodies as His spiritual life is linked with our spirits. The same life that is in the vine is in its branches; and in Christ, *"the true vine"* (John 15:1), there is both spiritual and bodily life. It is only by bringing into our bodies some of the same life that He is to bring at the resurrection that the Spirit *can* be the earnest of our inheritance to the body. Since our inheritance includes a glorified body, what must the earnest be? Thank God, *"the life also of Jesus* [may] *be made manifest in our mortal flesh"* (2 Cor. 4:11)—*immortal* life touching our *mortal* bodies with a foretaste of redemption, to enable us to finish our course, in order that we may *"receive a full reward"* (2 John 1:8).

Twelfth, does not nature itself reveal the present attitude of Christ toward the healing of our bodies? Nature everywhere is healing, or at least doing her best to heal. As soon as disease germs enter our bodies, nature begins to expel them. Break a bone, or cut a finger, and nature will do her utmost to heal, and usually succeeds. Now, has God commanded nature to rebel against His own will? If sickness is the will of God for His children, would it not seem that He has made such a command?

God's Use of Bodily Affliction

If sickness, as some think, is the will of God for His faithful children, then it is a sin for them even to desire to be well, to say nothing of spending thousands of dollars to defeat His purpose.

I truly thank God for all the help that has ever come to sufferers through physicians, surgeons, hospitals, and trained nurses; but if sickness is the will of God, then, to quote one writer, "Every physician is a lawbreaker; every trained nurse is defying the Almighty; every hospital is a house of rebellion, instead of a house of mercy," and, instead of supporting hospitals, we ought to do our utmost to close every one.

If the modern theology of those who teach that God wants some of His worshippers to remain sick for His glory is true, then Jesus, during His earthly ministry, never hesitated to rob the Father of all the glory He could by healing all who came to Him. The Holy Spirit, likewise, robbed Him of all the glory He could by healing all the sick in the streets of Jerusalem. And

Paul, too, robbed God of all the glory he could by healing all the sick on the island of Melita.

Many people today believe that God afflicts even the obedient, because He loves them, making sickness a love token from our heavenly Father. If this is true, why do they try to get rid of His love token? Why does the one suffering with cancer not pray for the second blessing for himself, and also ask Him to thus bless wife, children, father, mother, neighbors, and so forth?

Does God not sometimes chasten His people through sickness? Decidedly yes! When we disobey God, sickness may be permitted, through the Father's loving discipline; but God has told us just how it may be avoided and averted. *"If we would judge ourselves, we should not be judged. But when we are judged, we are chastened of the Lord, that we should not be condemned with the world"* (1 Cor. 11:31–32). These chastenings come to save us from final judgment; but when we see the cause of the chastening, and turn from it, God promises it will be withdrawn. As soon as *"we...judge ourselves,"* or learn our lesson, the absolute promise is that *"we* [shall] *not be judged."* By self-judgment, we may avoid chastening. Divine healing is not unconditionally promised to all Christians, regardless of their conduct. It is for those who believe and obey. *"All the paths of the LORD are **mercy** and truth unto **such** as keep his covenant and his testimonies"* (Ps. 25:10, emphasis added).

Next, His attitude now is shown by the fact that *"the Son of God was manifested, that he might destroy the works of the devil"* (1 John 3:8). Think of His leaving heaven and making the awful transition of becoming a man, and of all the suffering and sacrifice that followed. What was the purpose that moved Him in all this? The Scriptures give the answer: *"For this purpose,...that he might destroy the works of the devil"* (v. 8). This purpose includes the healing of *"all that were oppressed of the devil"* (Acts 10:38). Since His glorification, has He relinquished this purpose, which He retained even during the bloody sweat of Gethsemane and the awful tortures of Calvary? Does He want the works of the Devil that He formerly wanted to destroy to remain in our bodies? Can it be that He now wants cancer, a "plague" (Deut. 28:59, 61), a "curse" (see verses 15, 22, 27–29, 35, 59–61), or *"the works of the devil"* in *"the members of Christ"* (1 Cor. 6:15) and *"the temple[s] of the Holy [Spirit]"* (v. 19)? Is it not His will to heal any part of *"the body of Christ"* (1 Cor. 12:27)? If not, why has He commanded *"any sick"* in it to be anointed *in His name* for healing (James 5:14)?

Since *"the body is...for the Lord"* (1 Cor. 6:13), a *"living sacrifice...unto God"* (Rom. 12:1), would He not rather have a well body than one that is a wreck? If not, how can He make us *"perfect in every good work to do his will"* (Heb. 13:21)? Is God's expressed will—that we *"may abound to every good work"* (2 Cor. 9:8), be *"prepared unto every good work"* (2 Tim. 2:21), be *"thoroughly furnished unto all good works"* (2 Tim. 3:17), be *"zealous of good works"* (Titus 2:14), and be *"careful to maintain good works"* (3:8)—only for well men and women? If it is for everyone, He would have to heal the sick to make this possible, because no one can *"abound to every good work"* while confined to a sickroom.

Salvation All-Inclusive

Last, His present attitude is revealed in the very meaning of the word *salvation.* The Greek word for "salvation," *soteria,* implies deliverance, preservation, healing, health, soundness, and, in the New Testament, is sometimes applied to the soul and at other times to the body only. The Greek word *sozo,* translated "saved," also means "healed," "made sound," "made whole." In Romans 10:9, it is translated *"saved,"* and in Acts 14:9, the same word is translated *"healed"* in referring to the healing of the man lame from birth. Both Greek words for "salvation" and "saved" mean both spiritual and physical salvation; or, in other words, spiritual and physical healing. Paul, in Ephesians 5:23, stated, *"He is the Saviour of the body."*

Is this for some, or for all?

Dr. Scofield, in his footnote in the *Scofield Reference Bible* on the word *"salvation"* in Romans 1:16, wrote,

> "Salvation" is the great inclusive word of the Gospel, gathering into itself all the redemptive acts and processes: as justification, redemption, grace, propitiation, imputation, forgiveness, sanctification, and glorification.

The word *salvation,* therefore, includes our possession and enjoyment of all the blessings revealed by God's seven redemptive names; in fact, these names were given to show what our salvation includes. It is therefore the Gospel of healing for the body as well as for the soul that *"is the power of God unto salvation to every one that believeth; to the Jew first, and also to the Greek"* (Rom. 1:16). *"The same Lord over all is rich unto all that call upon him"* (Rom. 10:12).

An Indicative Comparison

The proofs of divine healing among those who say that they have been healed are not less bright and convincing than are the proofs of regeneration among those who today call themselves Christians. Are not those who testify that they have been healed in better health physically than many an equal number of Christians are spiritually? Would not the physical health of those who have been healed compare favorably with the spiritual health even of the average minister today? I think that the average Christian and even the average minister today are poorer proofs of the scriptural doctrine of regeneration than those who testify to healing are of the doctrine of healing; and yet the former have heard vastly more teaching as a basis for their faith for salvation.

Are all who have been baptized washed from *all* their sins? No! But those who have faith are; and what water is in the ordinance of Christian baptism, oil is in the ordinance of anointing the sick for healing.

Four

✦

The Lord's Compassion

Four

✦

The Lord's Compassion

The LORD is gracious, and full of compassion;
slow to anger, and of great mercy.
The LORD is good to all: and his
tender mercies are over all his works.
—Psalm 145:8–9

I n the study of the Lord's compassion, we have, to my
mind, a complete revelation of the Lord's willingness
to heal. During His earthly ministry, He was always
"moved with compassion" (see, for example, Matthew
14:14; Mark 1:41), and healed all *"that had need of
healing"* (Luke 9:11). It is *"this same Jesus"* (Acts 1:11)
who, after saying, *"It is expedient for you that I go
away"* (John 16:7), is now seated at the right hand of
God, *"that he might be a merciful* [compassionate] *and
faithful high priest"* (Heb. 2:17) for us.

In the Scriptures, "mercy" and "compassion"
mean the same thing. The Hebrew noun *rachamin*
is translated both *"mercy"* and *"compassion."* The
Greek verb *eleeo* is translated *"have mercy"* and *"have
compassion."* Likewise, the Greek adjective *eleemon* is
defined as "merciful" and "compassionate."

To have compassion is "to love tenderly, to pity, to
show mercy, to be full of eager yearning."

God Is Nothing as Much as Love

The text above begins with *"The LORD is gracious, and full of compassion."* These sentiments concerning the nature of God are expressed over and over throughout the Scriptures. God is not anything as much as He is love. The most conspicuous statements in the Scriptures about our heavenly Father are the declarations concerning His love, His mercy, His compassion. There is no note that can be sounded concerning God's character that will so inspire faith as this one. In our revivals, I have seen faith rise "mountain high" when the truth of God's present love and compassion began to dawn upon the minds and hearts of the people. It is not what God *can* do, but what we know He *yearns* to do, that inspires faith.

By always showing His compassion in the healing of the sick, Jesus unveiled the compassionate heart of God to the people, and the multitudes came to Him for help. Oh, how insidiously has Satan worked to hide this glorious fact from people. He has broadcasted the unscriptural, illogical, and worn-out statement that the age of miracles is past, until he has almost succeeded in eclipsing the compassion of God from the eyes of the world. Modern theology magnifies the power of God more than it magnifies His compassion, His power more than the great fact that *"the exceeding greatness of his power* [is] *to us-ward"* (Eph. 1:19). But the Bible reverses this, and magnifies His willingness to use His power more than it does the power itself. In no place does the Bible say that "God is power," but it does say that *"God is love"* (1 John 4:8, 16). It is not faith in God's power that secures His blessings, but faith in His love and in His will.

God's Love Veiled by Modern Theology

Again, the first statement in our text above is, *"The LORD is gracious,"* meaning, "He is disposed to show favors." This glorious fact, which shines with such brilliancy throughout the Scriptures, has been so eclipsed by modern theology that we hear everywhere that the Lord is *able* instead of *"the LORD is gracious."* Hundreds needing healing have come or written to us, saying, concerning their need of deliverance, "The Lord is able"; but their teaching, as well as their lack of teaching, has kept them from knowing that the Lord is willing. How much faith does it take to say, "The Lord is able"? The Devil knows that God is able, and he knows that God is willing; but he has kept the *people* from knowing the latter fact. Satan is willing to let us magnify the Lord's power, because he knows that this is not a sufficient basis for faith; but he knows the Lord's compassion and willingness is.

Before praying for the healing of people, we have to wait to teach them the Word of God until they can say, *"The LORD is gracious,"* instead of "The Lord is able." This is exactly what Jesus had to do before healing the leper who said, *"Lord, if thou wilt, thou canst make me clean"* (Matt. 8:2). Jesus showed His willingness, so that the man could really expect healing (v. 3).

In the previous chapter, many scriptural proofs of the Lord's present willingness to heal were presented. But even when we can advance from saying "He is able" to saying "He is willing," this is not enough. The word *willing* is too tame to fully express God's merciful attitude toward us. *"He **delighteth** in mercy"* (Mic. 7:18, emphasis added). We have His attitude more fully expressed in 2 Chronicles 16:9: *"For the eyes of the LORD run to and fro throughout the whole earth, to* *show himself strong in the behalf of them whose heart is perfect toward him."* This text reveals our Lord as being not only *willing,* but also *eager* to pour His blessings in great profusion upon all who make it possible for Him to do so. *"For the eyes of the LORD run to and fro,"* or, in other words, He is always hunting for opportunities to gratify His benevolent heart, because *"He delighteth in mercy."*

Benevolence is the great attribute of God; therefore, if you want to please Him, move the obstacles out of the way of the exercise of His benevolence. He is infinitely good, and He exists forever in a state of entire consecration to pour forth blessings upon His creatures whenever they make it possible, which all may do. Imagine that the vast Pacific Ocean were elevated high above us. Then imagine it poured out and pressing into every crevice to find an outlet through which it might stream its flood tides over all the earth, and you have a picture of God's benevolent attitude toward us.

Place Yourself Where God's Mercy Can Reach You

After first being properly enlightened, I challenge you to place yourself where God's mercy can reach you without His having to violate the glorious principles of His moral government; then wait and see if you don't experience the most overwhelming demonstration of His love and mercy. The blessing will flow until you have reached the limit of your expectation. Cornelius placed himself where God's mercy could reach him by saying to Peter, *"We [are] all here present before God, to hear all things that are commanded thee of God"* (Acts 10:33), and he found God's goodness so great that He could not wait for Peter to finish his sermon.

Just as soon as Peter had spoken enough to be a basis for their faith, down came the blessing. (See verses 1–48.)

Not only is God able, but He is also willing to do *"exceeding abundantly above all that we ask or think"* (Eph. 3:20). His love is so great that it could not be fully gratified by blessing all the holy beings in the universe; therefore, it is extended to His enemies *"throughout the whole earth"* (2 Chron. 16:9). It seems to me as if God would rather that we doubt His ability than His willingness. I would rather have a man who is in trouble say to me, "Brother Bosworth, I know you would help me if you could" (doubting my ability), than to say, "I know you can, but I have no confidence in your inclination to help me."

The text at the start of this chapter further states that *"the LORD is...full of compassion; slow to anger, and of great mercy."* When I think of how the Lord so floods our hearts with His tender love, until, in intercession for others, our hearts are too full of yearnings to express their feelings—yearnings that *"cannot be uttered"* (Rom. 8:26)—I stand in awe, and wonder what *His* compassion must be. A mother's compassion for her suffering child makes her not only willing to relieve the child, but also to suffer with him if she cannot relieve him. The Greek word *sumpathes,* translated *"having compassion,"* means "to suffer with another." Accordingly, Isaiah said, *"In all their affliction he was afflicted"* (Isa. 63:9). Is it not strange that this wondrous fact of God's mercy toward the sick, so clearly seen and applied during the darker ages of the Old Testament, should be overlooked and set aside in this "better" age, in which is opened the way for the fullest possible manifestations of His mercy toward every phase of human need?

The Benevolent Heart of God Reaches All

Our text, after showing the greatness of the Lord's compassion, closes with the logical conclusion, *"The LORD is good to **all**: and his tender mercies are over **all** his works."* In other words, He is so *"full of compassion"* that he cannot be a *"respecter of persons* ["exhibit partiality," Greek]*"* (Acts 10:34) in the bestowal of His mercies. How could He—who, being unable to fully gratify His benevolent heart by blessing holy beings, extends His mercies to the wicked of earth—withhold the common blessing of healing from any of His own obedient children?

What a strange doctrine is being taught today that the sick are not to look for as much mercy during this age of grace, which *"prophets and kings...desired to see"* (Luke 10:24), and *"angels desire to look into"* (1 Pet. 1:12), as sufferers did during the darker ages. Is God now more willing to show the mercy of forgiveness to the Devil's children than He is the mercy of healing to His own? The fact is, He loves His own sick and suffering child even more than He loves the sinner, and *"the mercy* [compassion] *of the LORD is from everlasting to everlasting* [not upon sinners alone, but also] *upon them that fear him"* (Ps. 103:17). *"Like as a father pitieth his children, so the LORD pitieth them that fear him"* (v. 13). *"As the heaven is high above the earth, so great is his mercy toward them that fear him"* (v. 11), as well as to the sinner. The sick Christian can say, with Solomon, *"There is no God like thee,...which keepest covenant, and showest mercy **unto thy servants**, that walk before thee with all their hearts"* (2 Chron. 6:14, emphasis added). Not some, but *"all the paths of the LORD are mercy and truth* [not unto His enemies, but] *unto such as keep his covenant and his testimonies"* (Ps. 25:10).

Instances of the Lord's Compassion

Now let us look at a few passages from the Gospels that show the Lord's compassion:

And there came a leper to him, beseeching him, and kneeling down to him, and saying unto him, If thou wilt, thou canst make me clean. And Jesus, moved with compassion, put forth his hand, and touched him, and saith unto him, I will; be thou clean. And as soon as he had spoken, immediately the leprosy departed from him, and he was cleansed....And they came to [Jesus] from every quarter.
(Mark 1:40–42, 45)

It was compassion that moved Christ to heal this leper.

Jesus...departed thence by ship into a desert place apart: and when the people had heard thereof, they followed him on foot out of the cities. And Jesus went forth, and saw a great multitude, and was moved with compassion toward them, and he healed their sick. (Matt. 14:13–14)

In this instance, as elsewhere, He was *"plenteous in mercy"* (Ps. 86:15) to all who *"had need of healing"* (Luke 9:11), and it was His compassion that moved Him.

And as they departed from Jericho, a great multitude followed him. And, behold, two blind men sitting by the way side, when they heard that Jesus passed by, cried out, saying, Have mercy on us, O Lord, thou son of David....And Jesus

81

stood still, and called them, and said, What will
ye that I shall do unto you? They say unto him,
Lord, that our eyes may be opened. So Jesus had
compassion on them, and touched their eyes: and
immediately their eyes received sight, and they
followed him.   (Matthew 20:29–30, 32–34)

These blind men asked for the *"mercy"* of having their
eyes opened, and Jesus granted to them the mercy of
healing, proving that healing, as well as forgiveness, is
a mercy. In those days, when the sick sought healing,
they asked for mercy. In our day, most people think of
mercy as applied only to the sinner, not knowing that
His mercy is also extended to the sick.

God, the Father of Mercies

Paul, who called God *"the Father of mercies"* (2
Cor. 1:3), proved this attribute of God by healing all
the sick on the island of Melita. (See Acts 28:1–9.)
Jesus said, *"Blessed are the merciful* [compassionate]:
for they shall obtain mercy" (Matt. 5:7). Job was healed
when he prayed for his friends. (See Job 42:7–10.)
In accordance with Matthew 5:7, Job obtained mercy
by showing it. Referring to, and accounting for, Job's
healing, James 5:11 says, *"The Lord is very pitiful,*
and of tender mercy," and follows with this direction
to the church:

Is any sick among you? let him call for the
elders of the church; and let them pray over
him, anointing him with oil in the name of the
Lord: and the prayer of faith shall save the sick,
and the Lord shall raise him up; and if he
have committed sins, they shall be forgiven him.
(James 5:14–15)

In other words, because *"the Lord is very pitiful, and of tender mercy,"* let *"any sick"* in the church today obtain their healing, as Job did. Having provided all we need, Jesus is still saying, as He did to the two blind men, *"What will ye that I shall do unto you?"* (Matt. 20:32).

Jesus had compassion on a man who lived among the tombs and was so possessed with a legion of demons that he cut himself with stones and broke the chains with which men tried to bind him. After Jesus had healed him, when he was clothed and in his right mind, he was so glad that he begged the Lord that he might remain with Him. (See Mark 5:2–18.)

> *Howbeit Jesus suffered him not, but saith unto him, Go home to thy friends, and tell them how great things the Lord hath done for thee, and hath had* **compassion** *on thee. And he departed, and began to publish in Decapolis how great things Jesus had done for him: and all men did marvel.*
> *(Mark 5:19–20, emphasis added)*

A Result of One Man's Testimony

And now let us read Matthew 15:30–31, and see the results of this one man's testimony, which he gave to proclaim the Lord's compassion.

> *And great multitudes* [in Decapolis] *came unto him, having with them those that were lame, blind, dumb, maimed, and many others, and cast them down at Jesus' feet; and he healed them: insomuch that the multitude wondered, when they saw the dumb to speak, the maimed*

*to be whole, the lame to walk, and the blind to
see: and they glorified the God of Israel.*

It was not their being sick, as some teach today,
but their being healed, that caused these *"great multitudes"* to glorify *"the God of Israel."* Oh, how much
glory would come to God, as well as how many blessings to the world, if every minister today would present clearly the biblical promises of healing to the sick,
and then, as soon as each one was healed, if he would,
in his turn, proclaim the Lord's compassion throughout his own "Decapolis"? In a short time, thousands
upon thousands everywhere who are now sick would
obtain faith in Christ for healing. It would then again
be said of the multitudes that they *"glorified the God
of Israel."*

The higher critic and the Modernist would soon
be unpopular, and the false healing cults would not
draw away from the church the multitudes who are
now being ensnared.

Not a Crime to Proclaim God's Goodness

Mark 5:20 states that this man began to *"publish
["proclaim,"* NJKV]*"* the Lord's compassion. Some people
oppose and write articles against us for publishing the
testimonies of those who are miraculously healed. What
is the matter? Is there anything wrong in obeying the
Lord's command to *"make known his deeds among the
people"* (1 Chron. 16:8; Ps. 105:1)? Since Jesus died to
open the way for His mercies to reach all the needs of
men, we surely ought to be willing for them to know
it. One would think, to read some of the books and articles that are being written, that it is a crime to let the
people know about the Lord's compassion.

You will notice in the various Scriptures quoted above that, as the result of Jesus' miracles of healing, *"his fame* [was] *spread abroad"* (Mark 1:28), *"and they came to him from every quarter"* (v. 45). The Scriptures say of the multitudes, *"They followed him on foot out of the cities"* (Matt. 14:13), and *"Great multitudes came unto him"* (Matt. 15:30). Multitudes, multitudes, multitudes everywhere!

It is the same today. Just as soon as it is known in any city that *"this same Jesus"* (Acts 1:11) is actually healing the sick—as soon as the command is obeyed to *"make known his deeds among the people,"* and His compassion is proclaimed—the people come *"from every quarter."* I have never seen anything that will so break down all the barriers and bring the people from every quarter as the manifestation of the Lord's compassion in healing the sick. We have found, in our revivals, that as soon as the public finds out what *"this same Jesus"* is doing, people come from the Methodist quarter, the Baptist quarter, the Catholic quarter, the Christian Science quarter, the Unity quarter, the Spiritualist quarter, the Jewish quarter, the poor man's quarter, the rich man's quarter, and from every quarter—and multitudes hear the Gospel and give their lives to God who would never even attend the meetings if there were no healing miracles to reveal His compassion.

The Results of Present-day Healings

If Christ and His apostles could not draw the multitudes without miracles, does He expect more from us? Instead of the "ministry of healing" diverting from the more important matter of salvation for the soul, I have seen more happy conversions through it in a single week than I ever saw in a whole year of evangelistic work during the thirteen years before the Lord led me to preach this part of the Gospel in a bolder and more public way. As soon as our revivals get under way, hundreds nightly crowd forward to give their hearts and lives to God, and whole cities begin talking about Jesus. Other evangelists who have visited our revivals are now proving this to be true in their own meetings.

In our last revival preceding the writing of this book, conducted in Ottawa, Canada, during the seven weeks of the meeting, six thousand came for healing and about twelve thousand for salvation. I doubt if there would have been more than one thousand for salvation had it not been for the miracles of healing that displayed the compassion of the Lord. The city and country were stirred as never before in their history, and the largest crowds that ever gathered under one roof for religious meetings in this capital city of Canada filled the newly built million-dollar auditorium—the largest building in the city. Attendance ran as high as eight thousand in a single service. Before leaving the city, we received many hundreds of written testimonies from those who were healed or being healed from almost every kind of disease and affliction. To God be all the glory!

Healing a Mighty Evangelistic Tool

One Baptist evangelist who, among other evangelists, is now proving this phenomenon to be true, has written, in one of ten pamphlets he has published on the subject, that healing is the greatest evangelizing tool that the Lord ever used, and that he would not return to the old (new) way for all the money in America.

Now let us look at another passage concerning the Lord's compassion:

> *And Jesus went about all the cities and villages, teaching in their synagogues, and preaching the gospel of the kingdom, and healing every sickness and every disease among the people. But when he saw the multitudes, he was moved with compassion on them, because they fainted, and were scattered abroad, as sheep having no shepherd. Then saith he unto his disciples, The harvest truly is plenteous, but the labourers are few; pray ye therefore the Lord of the harvest, that he will send forth labourers into his harvest. And when he had called unto him his twelve disciples, he gave them power against unclean spirits, to cast them out, and to heal all manner of sickness and all manner of disease....[Jesus] commanded them, saying,...Go, preach,...heal the sick. (Matt. 9:35–10:1, 5, 7–8)*

In this passage, we see that His compassion toward the sick was becoming so well known that the *"harvest"* had become too great for the One Reaper. His compassionate heart was full of yearning over the increasing numbers who could not reach Him because of the crowds. *"When he saw the multitudes, he was moved with compassion on them"* (Matt. 9:36). It was as if He was able to personally minister to only a portion of them, and His compassion for the rest of the rapidly growing multitudes was now moving Him to thrust forth other laborers to heal as well as to preach. *"**His** harvest"* (v. 38) is not only of the same nature in our day as it was then, but it is also much greater than when He was here; and, because His compassion is still the same, He wants the same kind of reapers to reap the same harvest, or results, by preaching and healing in *"all the cities and villages"* (v. 35).

His compassion, manifested through the twelve new laborers (His disciples), soon necessitated the thrusting forth of seventy more who were empowered to preach and to heal (Luke 10:1–9, 17–18). Laborers of this kind are few today, while *"the harvest"* truly is plenteous beyond what it was then. What the Lord was beginning *"to do and teach"* (Acts 1:1) is exactly what He wants done and taught everywhere in our day. Instead of *ending* something, which is the modern idea of His work, He was *starting* something that He promised to continue and increase. It was not the modern "gospel," but *"this gospel"* (Matt. 24:14), the Gospel that Christ proclaimed, that He said *"shall be preached in all the world"* (v. 14).

A Strange Reversal of Christ's Promise

Jesus, in John 14:12–13, emphatically taught and promised that the same mercy and compassion that He had for the multitudes when He lived on earth could reach people through our prayers while He is our High Priest in heaven. In fact, His departure was to open the way for His compassion to be manifested on a much larger scale. Isaiah prophesied of Him, *"Therefore will he be exalted, that he may have mercy"* (Isa. 30:18). Jesus said, *"It is expedient* [profitable] *for you that I go away"* (John 16:7). This could not be true if His going away would withdraw, or even modify, the manifestation of His compassion in healing the sick.

Is it not strange that many ministers today exactly reverse Christ's promise that the same and greater works will be done by teaching that the age of miracles is past? Others do the same by teaching that

God wants some of His devout children to remain sick for His glory, as well as many other traditional and unscriptural ideas.

Everyone who teaches that healing is not for all who need it today, as it was in the past, is virtually teaching that Christ's compassion toward the sick has at least been modified since His exaltation. Worse yet, others teach that His compassion in healing the sick has been entirely withdrawn. To me, it is a mystery how any minister can take a position that veils and interferes with the manifestation of the greatest attribute of Deity, God's compassion, which is divine love in action. When Paul wanted to make the strongest possible appeal for consecration, he said, *"I beseech you...by the **mercies** of God"* (Rom. 12:1, emphasis added), which are the manifestation of His greatest attribute.

Two Important Questions

Jesus said, *"When he, the Spirit of truth, is come,... he shall glorify me"* (John 16:13–14). Could the Spirit glorify Christ to the sick by telling them that the age of miracles is past, or that Jesus, since His exaltation, has withdrawn or modified His ministry to the sick, after He Himself promised that through Him we would do *"the works"* that He did, *"and greater works"* (John 14:12), during this age? Has the Spirit come to magnify Christ by modifying His ministry to His sick and suffering brothers while He is their High Priest— directly contrary to the glorifying of the God of Israel in Decapolis, occasioned by the healing of the multitudes? If so, then the not uncommon practice of praying for the sick to have fortitude and patience to bear their afflictions, instead of praying *"the prayer of faith"* (James 5:15) for their healing, is the right approach.

It was after He became our High Priest that He spoke from heaven seven times, saying, *"He that hath an ear, let him hear what the Spirit saith unto the churches"* (Rev. 2:7, 11, 17, 29; 3:6, 13, 22). Men are saying much today that the Spirit has *never* said, and which is the opposite of what He *does* say. The following are a few of the things that the Spirit says for the purpose of glorifying Christ.

Christ Is a Compassionate High Priest

"Wherefore in all things it behoved him to be made like unto his brethren, that he might be a merciful [compassionate] *and faithful high priest"* (Heb. 2:17).

We have already seen that both the words *merciful* and *compassionate* are given as the meaning of the Greek adjective *eleemon,* which is translated *"merciful"* in this passage. This verse has no reference to Christ's compassion as manifested during His earthly ministry; it refers only to His ministry from heaven, and to the fact that the purpose of His incarnation was so that He might show compassion as our High Priest after His return to heaven. *"All that Jesus began both to do and teach, until the day in which he was taken up"* (Acts 1:1–2) is what, because of His unchanging compassion, He promised would continue and be greater after He went away.

Christ Is Touched with the Feeling of Our Infirmities

The Spirit further glorifies Christ by saying that He is even now *"touched* [*sumpatheo,* Greek—translated *"had compassion"* in Heb. 10:34] *with the feeling of our infirmities"* (Heb. 4:15), that He still *"can have compassion"* (Heb. 5:2), and that He is *"Jesus Christ the same yesterday, and to day, and for ever"* (Heb. 13:8). Let us worship Him, because His compassion is the same today, and because, as He looks upon all our infirmities, He is still moved with compassion, and yearns to help us.

Of course, we recognize, and thank God, that many Christians who do not believe in divine healing *do* cooperate with the Spirit in these glorious sentiments as they pertain to the more important work of saving souls. Yet how wonderful it would be if all ministers and Christians, instead of saying that the age of miracles is past, would cooperate with the Spirit by also proclaiming to sufferers these glorious sentiments that the Spirit expresses while fulfilling His office-work of glorifying the exalted Christ. Instead of being priests and Levites "passing by on the other side" (see Luke 10:30–37), the church is commanded to be a "Good Samaritan," ministering with compassion to the physical needs of the sick and afflicted, binding up their wounds, pouring in the healing balm of wine and oil (the Word of God and the Spirit of God); for *"he sent his word, and healed them"* (Ps. 107:20) by the power of the Spirit. Jesus pronounced a woe upon the scribes and Pharisees for having *"omitted the weightier matters of...mercy, and faith"* (Matt. 23:23).

Christ in Heaven Is Moved with Compassion

In the fifth chapter of Acts, we have another wonderful proof that Christ's compassion toward the sick is still the same as it was when He lived on earth. We read, concerning the multitudes who were brought

into the streets of Jerusalem in the days after He
had ascended to the Father, that *"they were healed
every one"* (v. 16). Here again, as our High Priest in
heaven, Jesus did exactly what He did before going
away. From heaven, He was moved with compassion,
and He healed all who had need of healing.

Recall that even in the last chapter of Acts, we
find His compassion manifested from heaven by the
healing of all on the island of Melita (Acts 28:1–9).
While He is our High Priest, His compassion is so
great that He *"ever liveth to make intercession for* [us]"
(Heb. 7:25).

Again, His compassion for the sick, after He
was glorified, moved Him to *"set* [establish]...*in the
church"* (1 Cor. 12:28) the gifts of faith, of miracles,
and of healing for the recovery of the sick while He
is our High Priest throughout the centuries. (See 1
Corinthians 12:4–11; 28.) After Christ's exaltation, to
express it in the words of the Reverend W. C. Stevens,
"we find, as a matter of course *and of necessity,* 'gifts
of healing' taking just such rank and prominence as
they did in our Lord's personal ministry on earth."

Even Laymen May Pray for the Sick

Again, it is His present compassion for the sick
that caused Him, as our High Priest and Head of the
church, to command the elders, and even the laymen,
to pray *"the prayer of faith"* (James 5:15) for the healing of *"any sick"* (v. 14) during the church age. On this
point, the Reverend W. C. Stevens remarked,

> All preachers, teachers, writers, and others who
> hand out the Word of Life to the people, should
> keep this direction (James 5:14) as continuously

before the people as sickness itself constantly confronts them.

Even during His earthly ministry, our Lord, who is worthy of being adored, would make any sacrifice and suffer even the Curse itself, in order to open the way for His compassion to reach the most unworthy and the most provoking of His enemies. Both the bloody sweat of Gethsemane and the horrible tortures of Calvary were but the manifestations of His infinite compassion. He went to Calvary with "His face set like flint" (see Isaiah 50:7); for, after He had been betrayed by the kiss of Judas into the hands of His crucifiers, and Peter had cut off the ear of the servant of the high priest, Jesus healed the ear of His enemy, and told Peter to put up his sword. Christ sheathed, as it were, His own sword by holding in check the most natural impulse of His holy soul in refusing to pray when, by praying, He could have had, instantly, more than twelve legions of angels to enable Him to escape the agony of the cross (Matt. 26:53–54). But then there would have been only a judgment seat, and no mercy seat, for fallen man with all his needs of body, soul, and spirit.

In His substitutionary work for us, He anticipated every possible need of Adam's race, and opened the way for mercy to reach every phase of human need. He was then, and is now, moved with compassion toward all who need Him as the One who is Ever Present, Peace, Shepherd, Provider, Victor, Righteousness, and Physician, which are the seven blessings secured by the tragedy of His Cross, and revealed to us by His redemptive names. His covenants, including the covenant of healing, are given because of His mercy, and He *"keepeth covenant and mercy with them that love him and keep his commandments to a thousand generations"* (Deut. 7:9).

How Not to Grieve the Heart of Jesus

Doubting or ignoring His love and compassion grieves the heart of Jesus. It made Him weep over Jerusalem (Luke 19:41–44). So many times, in our day, ministers have said that we do not *need* miracles now, thinking that the Lord's miracles were only signs to prove His deity, and so forth. I have said to them, "If you had a cancer eating your head off, *you* would need a miracle, would you not?" Most people today are so in the dark on this subject that it never occurs to them that there is mercy for the sick also. They never think of the gifts of healing and miracles as being the manifestations of Christ's compassion, and that, hour after hour, and day after day, for three years, He healed all who came to Him *because of His compassion*. Are not the needs of sufferers today the same as they were in that day? And do they not need as much compassion as anyone ever did in the past?

When we think of the countless numbers of people who are in despair, suffering with such intense agony that death would be a mercy, and to whom the physicians, after doing their best, have been obliged to say, "I can do no more for you," how precious it is to know that Christ's compassion, at every moment, is still precisely the same as when it was manifested during the three years of His earthly ministry of love—a fact upon which we may absolutely rely.

We have seen that bodily healing is a mercy that Christ, who was the expression of the Father's will, everywhere bestowed upon all who sought it; and we have these plain declarations: the Lord is *"plenteous in mercy unto all them* [including the sick] *that call upon* [Him]" (Ps. 86:5), because His *"mercy endureth for ever"* (see, for example, 1 Chronicles 16:34; Psalm 106:1; Jeremiah 33:11) and is *"from everlasting to everlasting"* (Ps. 103:17). He is full of mercy *"over all his works"* (Ps. 145:9). Do these Scriptures not settle the matter? Instead of saying that the age of miracles is past, say, "It is written! It is written!"

Five

✦

How to Appropriate the Blessing of Bodily Healing

How to Appropriate the Blessing of Bodily Healing

(Author's Note: In this chapter, I am repeating a few of the statements made in previous pages, so that this one chapter may contain enough to lay a complete foundation for faith. This has been done for the benefit of some who may need the prayer of faith for their healing before they have time to read the entire book.)

The First Step in Receiving the Redemptive and Covenant Blessing of Bodily Healing

The first step toward being healed is the same as the first step toward salvation or any other blessing that God promises; that is, for the sick person to know what the Bible clearly teaches—that it *is* God's will to heal until one has lived out the allotted span of life. Each individual sufferer must be convinced by the Word of God that his or her healing is the will of God, for it is impossible to have real faith for healing as long as there is the slightest doubt as to its being God's will.

It is impossible to boldly claim by faith a blessing that we are not certain that God offers, because the

99

power of God can be claimed only where the will of God is known. For instance, it would be next to impossible to get a sinner to "[believe] *unto righteousness*" (Rom. 10:10) before you had fully convinced him that it was God's will to save him. Faith begins where the will of God is known. Faith must rest on the will of God alone, not on our desires or wishes. Appropriating faith is not faith that believes that God *can* but that He *will*. Those who claim to believe in healing, but say one word in favor of it and ten words against it, cannot produce faith for healing.

Faith Is Expecting God to Do

When God commands us to pray for the sick, He intends for us to pray with faith, which we could not do if we did not know His will in the matter. Until a person knows God's will, he has no basis for faith, because faith is expecting God to do what we know it is His will to do. It is not hard, when we have faith, to get God to do His will.

When we know it is His will, it is not difficult for us to believe that He will do what we are sure He wants to do. It is in this way that every saved person has experienced the still greater miracle of the new birth. There can be no appropriation by faith until we are caused to know by the Gospel what God has provided for us.

There is no doctrine more emphatically taught throughout the Word of God than that, through the atonement of Christ, both salvation and bodily healing were provided, and that it is God's will to take away the sickness of His own, and to fulfill the number of their days according to His promise (Exod. 23:25–26). As the types in Leviticus 14 and 15 show that it was invariably through atonement that sickness was healed under the Law of Moses, so Matthew 8:17 definitely states that Jesus healed all diseases on the ground of the Atonement. This Scripture shows us that Christ's reason for making no exceptions while healing the sick who thronged Him was His atonement, which He made for all of Adam's race, including you. As multitude after multitude pressed upon Him *"to hear him, and to be healed of their diseases"* (Luke 6:17), it is repeatedly stated throughout the Gospels that He healed them all. (See, for example, Matthew 4:24; 12:15; 14:14; Luke 4:40; Acts 10:38.) He could make no exceptions. Why? Because in His coming atonement, *"Himself took our infirmities, and bare our sicknesses"* (Matt. 8:17). Since it is *"our"* infirmities that He bore, it requires the healing of all to fulfill this prophecy. God carefully put this in such language that we would have to misquote it to leave ourselves out.

What Calvary provides is for all!

God's way of saving the soul, of healing the body, and of doing everything else He wants to do is to send His Word—His promise—and then keep the promise wherever it produces faith. Divine procedure in healing is stated in the text, *"He sent his word, and healed them, and delivered them from their destructions* [graves]*"* (Ps. 107:20). It is *"the word of God, which effectually worketh"* in those who believe (1 Thess. 2:13), and is *"health to all their flesh"* (Prov. 4:22).

Just as a little girl's faith for a new dress comes by hearing the promise of her mother to buy it the next Saturday, so our faith for healing comes by hearing God's Word, or promise, to do it. Both the little girl's faith and ours *"cometh by hearing"* (Rom. 10:17). Now, the little girl could not, and would not, be expected to have faith for a new dress until her mother promised it; in the same way, we cannot, nor are we expected to, have faith for healing or salvation or any other blessing until that faith comes by hearing the Word (promise) of God to do it.

How could anyone find justification by faith until it was preached to him, and how could anyone find healing by faith until it was preached to him? It is the Scriptures that are able to make men *"wise unto salvation"* (2 Tim. 3:15). We must see that the Creator and Redeemer of the body is also its Physician before we have reason to expect healing.

The Value of God's Redemptive Names

Now, since God heals us by sending His Word (Ps. 107:20), what can be more His Word than His redemptive and covenant names, which were given, all seven of them, for the specific purpose of revealing to every man in Adam's race His redemptive attitude toward them?

When Christ commands us to *"preach the gospel to every creature"* (Mark 16:15), He intends for us to tell the Good News of redemption. His seven redemptive names reveal what our redemption includes. He has many other names, but only seven *redemptive* names, and these seven names are never used in the Scriptures except in His dealings with man. There are not six names, or eight, but seven, the perfect number, because He is a perfect Savior, and His redemption covers the whole scope of human need. The blessings revealed by each of these names are all in the Atonement. For instance, JEHOVAH-SHAMMAH means *"The LORD is there"* (Ezek. 48:35), or present, *"made nigh by the blood of Christ"* (Eph. 2:13).

JEHOVAH-SHALOM is translated "The Lord Our Peace." This is in the Atonement because *"the chastisement of our peace was upon him"* (Isa. 53:5).

JEHOVAH-RA-AH is translated *"The LORD is my shepherd"* (Ps. 23:1). He became our Shepherd by giving His life for the sheep (John 10:11, 15). So, you see, this privilege is in the Atonement.

JEHOVAH-JIREH means "The Lord Will Provide" an offering (see Genesis 22:8)—Christ Himself being the Offering provided on Calvary.

He became JEHOVAH-NISSI, "The Lord our Banner," or "Victor," by *spoil*[ing] *principalities and powers"* on the cross (Col. 2:15).

He bore our sins and became JEHOVAH-TSIDKENU, *"THE LORD OUR RIGHTEOUSNESS"* (Jer. 23:6), opening the way for every sinner to receive the gift of righteousness.

JEHOVAH-RAPHA is translated *"I am the LORD that healeth thee"* (Exod. 15:26), or "I am the Lord your Physician." This also is in the Atonement, for *"Himself took our infirmities, and bare our sicknesses"* (Matt. 8:17).

This completes the list of the seven redemptive names, which were given for the purpose of revealing God's relationship toward us all under each of these seven titles. These seven names all belong abidingly to Christ, and it is under each of these seven titles that He is the same yesterday, today and forever (Heb. 13:8). Jesus says to all who come to Him for any of these seven blessings, *"Him that cometh to me I will in no wise cast out"* (John 6:37).

This is the Good News that God wants preached to every creature, so that every creature may have the privilege of enjoying *"the fulness of the blessing of the gospel of Christ"* (Rom. 15:29).

I say again that nothing is more God's Word *"settled in heaven"* (Ps. 119:89) than His redemptive name

JEHOVAH-RAPHA. No one has a right to change God's "I *am* JEHOVAH-RAPHA" to "I *was* JEHOVAH-RAPHA" because *"the word of the Lord endureth for ever"* (1 Pet. 1:25).

Since JEHOVAH-SHALOM, "The Lord Our Peace," is one of Christ's redemptive names, has not every man a redemptive right to obtain peace from Him? Has not every man, likewise, a redemptive right to obtain victory from JEHOVAH-NISSI? Has not every man a redemptive right to obtain *"the gift of righteousness"* (Rom. 5:17) from JEHOVAH-TSIDKENU, and so forth? If so, why has not every man a redemptive right to obtain healing from JEHOVAH-RAPHA?

This name, JEHOVAH-RAPHA, was so accepted and believed by those to whom it was first sent that *"there was not one feeble person among their tribes"* (Ps. 105:37); and whenever this state of health was interfered with by their transgressions, as soon as they repented, typical atonements were made, and God was still JEHOVAH-RAPHA, the Healer, not to some, but to all. God wants this redemptive name, as well as all the others, to be sent *"to every creature"* (Mark 16:15), with the promise that *"they shall recover"* (v. 18), for *"the Lord shall raise* [them] *up"* (James 5:15).

The Bronze Serpent a Type of Christ

God ratified this word to the dying Israelites by sending them the added word, *"Every one that is bitten, when he looketh upon it* [the bronze serpent—the type of Calvary], *shall live"* (Num. 21:8). If bodily healing is not provided in the Atonement, why were these dying Israelites required to look at the type of the Atonement for bodily healing? As their curse was removed by the lifting up of the type of Christ, so ours is removed by the lifting up of Christ, the Antitype. Since the Spirit is given to us to make Christ real, why should we not look to Christ Himself with as much expectation as they did to the type?

It will be well to note that they could not look at the bronze snake and their symptoms at the same time. Likewise, Abraham's faith became strong as he looked to the promise of God. Some people reverse this, and their faith becomes weak while they look at their symptoms and forget the promise. Since God healed by sending His Word, which is the only basis for our faith, we will miss healing if we allow our symptoms to hinder us from expecting what His Word promises.

The Second Step

The second step is to be sure you are right with God, because our redemptive blessings are conditional. After we hear the Gospel and know what it offers, Jesus says, *"Repent ye, and believe the gospel"* (Mark 1:15). Only those who are right with God can follow these instructions for healing. When seeking healing for our bodies, there should be no compromise with the Adversary of our souls, because it is he who is the author of our diseases. Jesus may, but He has not promised to, destroy the works of the Devil in our bodies while we are clinging to the works of the Devil in our souls. It is hard to exercise faith for the removal of one part of the Devil's work while we allow a worse part to remain.

Until a person squarely faces and settles the question of obedience to God, he is not on believing ground. Psalm 66:18 says, *"If I regard iniquity in my heart, the Lord will not hear me."* It is when our hearts do not condemn us that we have confidence toward God (1 John 3:21). James says, *"Confess your faults one to another,...that ye may be healed"* (James 5:16). It is

God's will *"that thou mayest prosper and be in health, even as thy soul prospereth"* (3 John 1:2).

The command for the sick to *"call for the elders"* (James 5:14) was first written to Christians who had been filled with the Spirit. There is something wrong when a person desires the blessing but not the Blesser—His mercy but not Himself. It is not proper to seek His mercy while rejecting His will. Do not ask for a little blessing while rejecting a big one. It is impossible to receive and reject divine blessings at the same time.

God is waiting to say to Satan and disease what He said to Pharaoh: *"Let my people go, that they may **serve** me"* (Exod. 7:16, emphasis added). "Our first consideration," said the Reverend P. Gavin Duffy, "in all things, even in asking for the restoration of bodily health, should be the glory of God."

Strength for service to God is the only proper basis of approach when seeking health at His hand. The anointing with oil for healing is, itself, a symbol and sign of consecration.

We must desire our health for God's glory. The Reverend R. A. Torrey said,

> What, then, does the anointing mean? Turn to Leviticus 8:10–12, and you get God's answer to the question. *"And Moses took the anointing oil, and anointed the tabernacle and all that was therein, and sanctified them,"* that is, he *set them apart for God.* The anointing *"with oil in the name of the Lord"* (James 5:14) was an act of dedication and consecration, implying on the part of the one anointed a full surrender to God of his hands to work for Him and for Him alone, of his feet to walk for Him and Him alone, his eyes to see, his lips to speak, his ears

to hear for Him and Him alone, and his whole
body to be the temple of the Holy Spirit.

*"Beloved, I wish above all things that thou mayest
prosper and be in health, even as thy soul prospereth"*
(3 John 2).

The Holy Spirit tells us to submit ourselves to
God before He says to *"resist the devil"* (James 4:7),
because no one can successfully resist the Devil until
he submits himself to God. When the Devil is thus
resisted, he will not merely walk away; he will literally *run—"flee from you"* (v. 7).

The curse, including the different diseases catalogued in Deuteronomy 28, came upon the people
because their obedience and their service was not
"with joyfulness, and with gladness of heart" (v. 47).
The condition of heart that was responsible for the
coming of the diseases mentioned in the chapter is not
the condition for their removal. In other words, the
condition of heart that was responsible for the curse
in that day is not the condition of heart in which to
come to Him for the removal of the curse in our day.

God's Promises Only for the Obedient

It is to those who will delight themselves in the
Lord that He gives the desires of their hearts (Ps.
37:4). God has not lowered the standard for the day of
grace. It is only to the obedient—those who will *"dili-
gently hearken to the voice of the LORD"* and *"do that
which is right in his sight"* (Exod. 15:26)—that it is
said, *"The LORD will take away from thee all sickness"*
(Deut. 7:15). The Reverend Duffy also said,

Faith, you see, is the union of our hearts and
wills with God's will and purpose; and where

this unity is lacking results are impossible. This is a *very important spiritual law,* to which, in our times, we have been woefully blind.

God says, of fearing the Lord and departing from evil, *"It shall be health* ["medicine," Hebrew] *to thy navel, and marrow* ["moistening," Hebrew] *to thy bones"* (Prov. 3:7–8).

Faith always implies obedience. Paul wrote to the Ephesians to obey the first commandment, *"that it may be well with thee, and thou mayest live long on the earth"* (Eph. 6:3). Naaman's surrender and obedience to the Word of God was complete before he was healed. (See 2 Kings 5:1–14.)

It is to those who *"walk uprightly"* that it is said, *"No good thing will he withhold"* (Ps. 84:11). Therefore, before seeking anything from God, we should yield ourselves to the *"first and great commandment"* (Matt. 22:38): *"Thou shalt love the Lord thy God with all thy heart, and with all thy soul, and with all thy mind"* (v. 37). For God says, *"Because he hath set his love upon me, therefore will I deliver him"* (Ps. 91:14). He *"keepeth covenant and mercy with them that love him and keep his commandments to a thousand generations"* (Deut. 7:9). Therefore, like the leper, let us come and worship Him when asking for healing (Matt. 8:2–3).

"Length of days is in [Wisdom's] *right hand; and in her left hand riches and honour"* (Prov. 3:16). Marry Wisdom, and you get her possessions (vv. 13–18). Wisdom is represented in this passage as a bountiful queen, reaching forth blessings with both hands to all who will become subject to her government.

It is for *"them whose heart is perfect toward him"* that *"the eyes of the Lord run to and fro throughout the whole earth, to show himself strong"* (2 Chron. 16:9).

"A sound heart is the life of the flesh: but envy the rottenness of the bones" (Prov. 14:30). An unsound heart is worse than an unsound stomach, a diseased soul worse than a diseased body. A disordered will is worse than a disordered liver. Paul said, *"The body is… for the Lord"* before he said, *"The Lord* [is] *for the body"* (1 Cor. 6:13).

The Bible teaches that we are *"bought with a price: therefore glorify God in your body, and in your spirit, which are God's"* (v. 20). *"I beseech you therefore, brethren, by the mercies of God, that ye present your bodies a living sacrifice,…which is your reasonable service"* (Rom. 12:1). Therefore, present your body to Him if you want it healed. It is not until after it becomes His property that He promises to repair it.

First to the Cross for Cleansing

Bryant has said,

> The sure way for the sick is, first to the cross for cleansing, then to the Upper Room for the gift of the Spirit, then to the mount appointed for a life commission, and, lastly, to the Great Physician for strength for service.

> *If the Spirit of him that raised up Jesus from the dead dwell **in** you, he that raised up Christ from the dead shall also quicken your mortal bodies by his Spirit that dwelleth **in** you.*
> *(Rom. 8:11, emphasis added)*

In Christ, *"the true vine"* (John 15:1), there is all the life for our souls and bodies that we need. But how are we to possess and enjoy this life except by our union with the Vine? It is not apart from Him, but in Him, that *"ye are complete"* (Col. 2:10).

Substitution without union is not sufficient for our possession and enjoyment of the life of the Vine. If you need a miracle, get in tune with the Miracle Worker. We enjoy the life of the Vine by our perfect union with the Vine. Asking for healing while refusing to be led by the Spirit is like asking a carpenter to repair the house while refusing to let him in the house.

"As many as touched [Him] *were made perfectly whole"* (Matt. 14:36). You cannot touch Him with reservation; therefore, like the woman who pressed through the crowd and touched Him (see Luke 8:43–48), you must "elbow" out of your way, and press beyond, self-ishness, disobedience, unconfessed sins, lukewarm-ness, public opinion, traditions of men, articles written against divine healing—in fact, you must often press beyond your own pastor, who may be unenlightened in this part of the Gospel—press beyond doubts, double-mindedness, symptoms, feelings, and the lying Serpent.

The Holy Spirit, who is sent to execute for us the blessings of redemption, is our Paraclete, or Helper, and is ready to help us to press through and beyond all of these obstacles to the place where we can touch Him for our needs. God is waiting to pour out the Holy Spirit in fullness upon us. He comes as Christ's Executive to execute for us all the blessings provided by Calvary, and which are pledged to us in His seven redemptive and covenant names.

It is still true that as many as touch Him are made whole. How do we touch Him? By believing His prom-ise. This is an infallible way of touching Christ for anything He has promised. We touch Him by asking, and by believing that He hears our prayers when we pray. When the woman touched Him, it was her faith that made her whole, not a mere physical touch (Luke 8:48); for *"the flesh profiteth nothing"* (John 6:63), *"but the Spirit giveth life"* (2 Cor. 3:6). Millions of sinners have thus touched Him for the yet greater miracle of the new birth.

Not Mere Contact, but Union

As the sick touched Christ and were made whole when He walked upon the earth, so, now, it is the privilege of all actually to touch Him, and the touch now unites us to Christ in a closer union than it did then. This is not mere contact, but union as real as a branch and a vine. All that is in the Vine, including both spiritual and physical life, belongs to us—the branches.

The touch by faith can now bring us under the full control of the Holy Spirit, who is the Miracle Worker, as it could not do during Christ's earthly ministry, for the Spirit *"was not yet given"* (John 7:39). Jesus is no less a Savior and Healer since being glorified; He is *greater.* The privilege of touching Him now is much greater than when He was here in person, because more can now be received by the touch. From God's right hand, He has more to give; therefore, He said, *"It is expedient* [profitable] *for you that I go away"* (John 16:7). Since the Spirit comes to reveal Christ as He could not be revealed before He went away to send the Spirit, why can we not approach Christ for healing now with at least as much faith as those who thronged Him in that day?

The preceding shows the great importance of being right with God before asking for healing. The blessing of being right with God is a thousand times more desirable and enjoyable than the healing itself. I have seen the afflicted in body radiantly happy; but sinners in perfect health have been so unhappy as to commit suicide.

The Third Step

I will now endeavor to make plain how to *appropriate,* or take hold of, healing. Getting things from God is like playing checkers, when, after one person moves, he has nothing to do until the other player moves. Each person moves in his own turn. Similarly, when God has provided healing, or any other blessing, and sent us His Word, it is our move before He will move again. Our move is to expect what He promises when we pray, which will cause us to act on our faith before we see the healing, because the healing comes in the next move, which is God's move.

God never moves out of turn, but He always moves when it is His turn. When Noah was *"warned of God of things not seen as yet"* (Heb. 11:7), his move was to believe that the flood was coming and to act on his faith by building the ship on dry land. Therefore, when God says to *"any sick"* (James 5:14), *"The prayer of faith shall save the sick, and the Lord shall raise him up"* (v. 15), you, like Noah, are informed by God *"of things not seen as yet,"* and your move is the same as Noah's, which is to believe and act accordingly. Fallen nature is governed by what it sees, by its senses; but faith is governed by the pure Word of God, and is nothing less than expecting God to do what He promises—treating Him like an honest Being.

By *expectation,* I do not mean "hope." One writer has well said, "We hope for what *may* be possible, but we expect what *must* be possible...with that expectancy that shuts out doubt or fear of failure, and shows unshakable confidence."

Faith never waits to *see* before it believes, because it *"cometh by hearing"* (Rom. 10:17) about *"things not seen as yet"* (Heb. 11:7), and is *"the evidence of things not seen"* (v. 1). All that a man of faith needs is to know that God has spoken. This imparts perfect certainty to the soul. "Thus saith the Lord" settles everything. "It is written" is all that faith needs.

Faith always blows the ram's horn before, not after, the walls are down. (See Joshua 6:5, 15–20.) Faith never judges according to the sight of the eyes, because it is *"the evidence of things not seen"* but promised. Faith rests on far more solid ground than the evidence of the senses, and that is the Word of God, which *"abideth for ever"* (1 Pet. 1:23). Our senses may deceive us, but God's Word never does!

When the little girl is promised a new dress next Saturday, faith is the actual expectation that she has and manifests between now and Saturday. When Saturday comes, and she sees the new dress, faith for the new dress stops. Now, real faith always has corresponding actions. The little girl, because of her faith, claps her hands and says, "Goody! Goody! I am going to have a new dress next Saturday!" and runs to tell her playmates that she has the answer to her request.

God Cannot Lie

Jesus, at the grave of Lazarus, looked up and said, *"Father, I thank thee that thou **hast** heard me"* (John 11:41, emphasis added), though Lazarus was still dead. The little girl is not afraid to testify in advance that she is to have a new dress; and when her playmates say, "How do you know you are?" she confidently replies, "Why, Mamma promised it!" Now, you have a better reason for expecting healing than the little girl has for expecting a new dress, because the mother may die before Saturday, but God cannot. The mother can lie, but God cannot. The house may burn down with the mother's money. But every case of faith in history was a well-grounded assurance, produced by the promise of God alone and acted upon before there was anything visible to encourage the assurance, as with the little girl, "between now and Saturday."

Faith looks *"not at the things which are seen"* (2 Cor. 4:18). There was no flood in sight when Noah built his ark. And in Joshua's case, stone walls had never before fallen down at the blowing of rams' horns and shouting. The Israelites were merely expecting what God promised; and when they acted on their faith by blowing the rams' horns while the walls were still up, this was *their* move. Then, of course, God moved, in His turn, and down came the walls!

The whole eleventh chapter of Hebrews was written to show how each one who had faith acted "between now and Saturday." God is so well pleased with the actions of faith that he has listed in detail many such cases in this Faith Chapter. *"By faith Noah..."* (v. 7). *"By faith Jacob..."* (v. 21). *"By faith Joseph..."* (v. 22). *"By faith Moses..."* (vv. 23, 24). *"By faith the walls of Jericho fell down"* (v. 30). When everything seemed contrary to what God had promised, *"by faith Abraham..."* (vv. 8, 17). It was by considering the promise of God (not her barrenness) that Sarah received strength to become a mother *"when she was past age"* (v. 11).

These all acted with nothing but the Word of God as their reason for expecting the thing He had promised.

It is the same with every case of faith in history.

Jonah's symptoms were very real when he was inside the fish, and he did not deny them, but called them *"lying vanities"* (Jonah 2:8). In other words, any symptoms that make us doubt the fact that God is *"plenteous in mercy unto all them that call upon* [Him]" (Ps. 86:5) should be regarded as *"lying vanities."* Jonah said, *"They that observe lying vanities forsake their own mercy"* (Jonah 2:8). Instead of listening to Satan and watching our symptoms, we must be *"workers together with* [God]" (2 Cor. 6:1), who heals by sending His Word and keeping it!

We must cooperate with God by being occupied not with what the Devil says, but with the Word He sends for our healing.

Symptoms May Linger

Even when we do act on our faith, symptoms do not always disappear instantly. After Hezekiah was healed, it was three days before he was strong enough to go up to the house of the Lord. (See 2 Kings 20:1–5.) In John 4, the nobleman *"believed the word that Jesus had spoken unto him"* (v. 50), and when he met his servants, he inquired of them the hour when his dying son *"began to amend"* (v. 52).

The Bible differentiates between the *"gifts of healing"* and the gift of *"the working of miracles"* (1 Cor. 12:9). Christ could do no *miracle* in Nazareth because of the people's unbelief, but He healed a few sick ones (Mark 6:1–6). If everyone were to be made perfectly whole instantly, there would be no place for the gifts of healing; it would be all miracles. Many people miss healing by trying to confine God to miracles. Christ's promise is that *"they shall recover"* (Mark 16:18), but He does not say "instantly."

"Faith means that we are confident of what we hope for, convinced of what we do not see" (Heb. 11:1 MOFFATT). We are *"convinced,"* of course, because God, who cannot lie, has spoken. How all-sufficient is this reason for believing! Faith is, therefore, most rational. It is not, as many unthinking persons suppose, believing without evidence, but believing because of the very highest possible evidence, God's Word, which is *"settled in heaven"* (Ps. 119:89). The apostle James said, *"I will show you by my deeds what faith is!"* (James 2:18 MOFFATT). Faith, therefore, is being so convinced of the absolute truth of the declarations of God that are recorded in the Bible that we act on them.

Faith Is Both Rational and Safe

What can be more rational, and what can be more safe and certain?

Faith means to receive the written promise of God as His direct message to us. His promise means the same as if He appeared and said to us, "I have heard your prayer." The Word of God is made life to our bodies in exactly the same way that it is made life to our souls, which is by our believing His promise.

I have known some who had prayed for healing for as long as forty years without receiving it; and then, as soon as they were told how to appropriate healing, their healing has come sometimes in a moment. We do not have to pray for forty years, or for one week, for the blessing that Christ is eager to bestow. His compassionate heart yearns to heal us more than we have the capacity to desire it; but we keep Him waiting until we have the faith that *"cometh by hearing"* (Rom. 10:17), and act on that faith, because God will not cheat and move out of turn.

Appropriating by Faith

After seeing that Jesus bore our diseases as well as our sins on the cross, and therefore that we need not bear them, our next step is to appropriate by faith, which is the only scriptural way. The truth of the matter is, God gave us this part of our inheritance nearly 2,000 years ago, and He is the One who is waiting—waiting for us to appropriate the blessing by faith. Two thousand years ago, God *"put away sin"* (Heb. 9:26). Two thousand years ago, God *"laid on* [Christ] *the iniquity of us all"* (Isa. 53:6). Two thousand years ago, *"*[Christ] *took our infirmities, and bare our sicknesses"* (Matt. 8:17). God is the waiting party, waiting for us to be shown how to appropriate the blessing He has already given. *"The Lord is not slack* [slow] *concerning his promise,...but is longsuffering to us-ward"* (2 Pet. 3:9). Or, as Weymouth translates it, *"The Lord is not slow about His promise....He bears patiently with you."* In other words, He is not slow concerning His promises, but we are slow, and He is patient with us.

Most of us could have been saved five years earlier than we were. God was not making us wait, but we were making Him wait. It is the same with our healing.

"When Ye Pray," Not Afterward

Now, in Mark 11:24, Jesus tells us exactly how to appropriate any of the blessings purchased for us by His death. Having promised all that we need, He says, *"What things soever ye desire, when ye pray"*—not after you pray twenty years, not after you get well, but while you are still sick—*"when ye pray, believe that ye receive them, and ye shall have them."*

The condition of receiving what we ask God for is to believe that He answers our prayers when we pray, and that we *"shall recover,"* according to His promise (Mark 16:18).

In other words, when you pray for healing, Christ authorizes you to consider your prayer answered, as when He stood at the grave of Lazarus and said, *"Father, I thank thee that thou **hast** heard me"* (John 11:41, emphasis added), before He saw Lazarus come forth from the grave. When we ask for healing, Christ tells us to say, with faith, *"Father, I thank thee that thou **hast** heard me,"* before we have yet seen the answer to our prayer.

When God's Word alone is our reason for believing that our prayer is answered, before we see or feel it, this is faith!

Someone has written,

> Jesus declared, *"The **words** that I speak unto you, **they** are spirit, and they are life"* (John 6:63, emphasis added). John says, "The Word is God." (See John 1:1.) To receive the written words of Christ as the direct message to us is faith. This is the way the Word of God becomes life to us, both in our healing and in our salvation. For instance, the act of believing and receiving Christ according to John 1:12 is synonymous with the act of God that gives us, by His power, the new birth. By this same process also is divine healing imparted to our bodies.

Another writer has said, in substance, that, as with the woman who touched the hem of Christ's garment and was healed, faith, fact, and then feeling is the order of healing that God never departs from. If we depart from this order, neither faith, fact, nor feeling will be as we desire, because they will not be as God desires.

First Thessalonians 2:13 says that it is the Word of God that *"effectually worketh also in you that believe."* When His Word convinces us that our prayers are answered, before we have yet seen the answers, the Word begins to *"effectually"* work in us.

Harriet S. Bainbridge has written,

> God's Word never fails to work in those who accept it as such, because they are not entertaining doubts as to its being fulfilled in their own experiences....God has given all His blessings to Faith; He has none left to bestow upon unbelief.

When people say to me, "I do not know that it is God's will to heal me," I ask them, "Is it God's will to keep His promise?" If we are right with God, we should not consider *ourselves* any more than we would when men make promises to us. We should not ask ourselves, "Do *I* have faith enough?" but, "Is He honest?" It is not a question of how we feel, but of what are the facts. If the little girl whom I have been using as an example should get sick the next day, and feel bad, that has nothing to do with her mother buying her the new dress on Saturday. The Scriptures say, *"If we ask any thing according to his will, he heareth us"* (1 John 5:14). Is this true or not?

Does God answer prayer?

If you will steadfastly *"believe that ye receive"* (Mark 11:24) the answer to your prayer, and act on your faith, every one of you will be healed, though not always instantly—unless, of course, your allotted span of life has been lived out.

God always moves after our move, which is the acting out of a *"full assurance"* (Heb. 10:22), produced solely by His promise, before we see the answer to our prayer. Since healing is by faith, and *"faith without works is dead"* (James 2:20, 26), it is when we begin to *act on* our faith that God begins to heal.

Our Faith Makes God Act

Our *"work of faith"* (2 Thess. 1:11) sets God to working.

Now, we cannot all act in faith in the same way. As the ten lepers went to show themselves to the priests, they were healed. (See Luke 17:12–14.) Jonah, when inside the fish, could not go anywhere, but he did act on his faith by saying, while still in the fish, *"I will sacrifice unto thee with the voice of thanksgiving"* (Jonah 2:9). Acting on our faith by praising and thanking God in advance has been, throughout history, His appointed way for our appropriation of all His blessings. Hebrews 13:15 teaches us that our thank offering—our *"sacrifice of praise"*—is to be offered in advance for the blessing that God has promised, and that therefore we expect.

Psalm 50:14–15, says, *"Offer unto God thanksgiving; and pay thy vows unto the most High: and call upon me in the day of trouble: I will deliver thee, and thou shalt glorify me."* Here, as elsewhere, we are required to offer thanksgiving while we are still in trouble, as Jonah did. Perhaps this was the very promise he claimed. *"Let the poor and needy praise*

thy name" (Ps. 74:21); that is, praise God in advance
while you are still in need. *"Let us come before his
presence with thanksgiving"* (Ps. 95:2) does not mean
to get healed and then go from His presence thanking
Him, but to come to Him with thanksgiving for healing before being healed. *"**Enter into** his gates with
thanksgiving, and **into** his courts with praise"* (Ps.
100:4, emphasis added). We should also go away with
thanksgiving, but this is not faith.

Faith is what we have before we are healed. *"They
shall praise the LORD that **seek** him"* (Ps. 22:26, emphasis added). *"Thou shalt call thy walls Salvation, and
thy gates Praise"* (Isa. 60:18). Without praise, we are
up against a solid wall with no gate; but when we begin
praising and appropriating, we open our own gate and
walk through. The Scriptures say, *"Be glad and rejoice:
for the LORD **will do** great things"* (Joel 2:21, emphasis
added). Accordingly, after Christ ascended, the disciples *"were continually in the temple, praising and
blessing God"* (Luke 24:53)—not after, but *before* they
were filled with the Holy Spirit. It was *"when* [the Isra-
elite trumpeters and singers] *lifted up their voice...and
praised the LORD"* that *"the glory of the LORD...filled the
house of God"* (2 Chron. 5:13–14). *"Then believed they
his words* [not their symptoms, not the Father of Lies];
they sang his praise" (Ps. 106:12).

Make Satan Listen to Your Praises

Instead of your listening to the Father of Lies,
make *him* listen to your praising God for His promise!

"Let every thing that hath breath praise the LORD"
(Ps. 150:6). The sick man has breath. In other words,
while you are still sick, praise Him because you are
going to recover according to His promise. *"Let not*

your heart be troubled" (John 14:1, 27). *"In nothing be anxious* [distracted]; *but in everything by prayer and supplication with thanksgiving let your requests be made known unto God"* (Phil. 4:6 RV). *"Casting all your care upon him; for he careth for you"* (1 Pet. 5:7).

Every sick Christian, while sick, has a thousand times more to be happy over than the most cheerful sinner in perfect health.

Praise God because *"faith without works is dead"* (James 2:20, 26). *"In every thing give thanks: for this is the will of God in Christ Jesus concerning you"* (1 Thess. 5:18). *"I will bless the LORD at all times: his praise shall continually be in my mouth"* (Ps. 34:1). Since everything that has breath is commanded to praise the Lord, the only scriptural excuse for not praising Him is to be out of breath. *"By him therefore let us offer the sacrifice of praise to God continually, that is, the fruit of our lips giving thanks to his name"* (Heb. 13:15). *"Whoso offereth praise glorifieth me"* (Ps. 50:23). *"Because thy lovingkindness is better than life, my lips shall praise thee"* (Ps. 63:3). Praise Him because *"it is a good thing to give thanks unto the LORD"* (Ps. 92:1). *"Give thanks at the remembrance of his holiness"* (Ps. 30:4; 97:12). Praise Him because to withhold praise will show either unbelief or ingratitude. Praise Him because *"praise is comely for the upright"* (Ps. 33:1). Praise Him because God inhabits the praises of His people (Ps. 22:3). Paul and Silas sang praises at midnight with their backs bleeding and their feet in the stocks, and God sang bass with an earthquake, which set them free. (See Acts 16:22–39.)

Real faith rejoices in the promise of God as if it had already experienced the deliverance and was enjoying it.

When three great armies rose up against Jehoshaphat and the Israelites, which, humanly speaking, would mean annihilation, the Levites praised the Lord *"with a loud voice on high"* (2 Chron. 20:19), even when the only evidence that their prayer was answered was the naked Word of God, and *that* only through human lips (vv. 14–18). The next day, when the Israelites went out to the battle and *"began to sing and to praise"* (v. 22), the Lord, in His turn, moved and set ambushments against the enemy, and the victory was won (vv. 20–27). *"We have also a more sure word of prophecy,"* for *"holy men of God spake as they were moved by the Holy Ghost"* (2 Pet. 1:19, 21).

Thomas à Kempis has written,

> As in Eden the Enemy succeeded in making void God's testimony as to the results of eating the forbidden fruit, so now he seeks to make void God's testimony as to the results of believing the Gospel. After God said, "In the day thou eatest thereof thou shalt surely die," the Serpent said, "Thou shalt not surely die," and now, when God's Word plainly says, "They shall lay hands on the sick and they *shall* recover," the same Serpent seeks to persuade them that they shall *not* recover. Is it rational to believe the "father of lies" in preference to the Son of God, who is Incarnate Truth? When coming to God for salvation or healing, it is essential for each one to decide whether he shall allow the hiss of the Serpent to rise above the voice of God.
>
> Blessed are the ears that hear the pulses of the divine whisper, and give no heed to the many whisperings of the world.

When, after you have been anointed for healing, Satan tells you that you will not recover, say to him, as Jesus did, *"It is written"* (Matt. 4:4, 7, 10). Say, "It is written, *'They shall recover'* (Mark 16:18), and *'The Lord shall raise him up'* (James 5:15)." Also, in the passage from James, *"anointing him with oil in the name of the Lord"* (v. 14) means the same as if the Lord Himself anointed you. Expect Him to honor His own ordinance and His own promise.

Why Listen to the Devil?

All that the Devil heard from the lips of Christ when he tempted Him was, *"It is written,...It is written,...It is written."* *"Then the devil leaveth him"* (Matt. 4:11). But all we hear from some people is, "The Devil says,...The Devil says,...The Devil says," as though Christ's words were of less consequence than those of the Devil! Christ's way was to quote the Word of God, and it is the most successful way of resisting the Devil. Let us not try another! *"Neither give place to the devil"* (Eph. 4:27). *"Resist the devil, and he will flee from you"* (James 4:7).

There is just one way of resisting the Devil, and that is by steadfastly believing and acting upon God's Word. Whenever we are affected by any other voice more than the voice of God, we have forsaken the Lord's way for our healing.

What reason do you have for doubting? You have no more reason for doubting than the sinner has when he repents and asks for forgiveness for his sins. You have exactly the same reason for expecting to be healed that you had for expecting to be saved. Duffy said, "You have His Word for it, and if you cannot accept that to the point of acting upon it, then your faith is still very far from what it should be."

The Lord's Compassion a Basis for Faith

What a basis for faith is the Lord's compassion! Since Christ has redeemed us from sickness, surely His love and faithfulness may be trusted. The Cross is a sure foundation and a perfect reason for the exercise of faith.

Someone has said,

> Let us put our sickness away by faith, as we would put away sin. The consecrated Christian will not consciously tolerate sin for a moment, and yet how tolerant some are toward sickness. They will even pet and indulge their aches and pains, instead of resisting them as the works of the Devil.

Harriet S. Bainbridge said, in essence, that the Lord Jesus has declared, concerning the sin, sorrow, and physical misery of Adam's race, *"It is finished"* (John 19:30), and He has offered to each one of us the gift of the Holy Spirit to enable us to realize and enjoy the great salvation He purchased for us. To believe without doubt that Christ's words *"It is finished"* are a literal statement of an unchangeable fact invariably brings deliverance.

The Serpent is still denying this great saying of Christ, to our great loss, just as he caused Eve to forget and disregard words that God had plainly spoken to her. When we realize that our redemption from sickness was actually accomplished in the body of our crucified Lord, and when we wholeheartedly believe and receive what God declares in His written Word about the matter, then the Holy Spirit gives us the personal experience of Christ as our Physician.

Present-day Results of Believing God

Following these instructions has brought soundness to thousands who had before been taught that the age of miracles is past, that God wants people to remain sick for His glory, and so forth. Those who were born blind are now seeing; those who were deaf and mute from birth are now hearing and speaking; those who were crippled from birth are now perfectly whole; those who had been epileptics for years are now free and rejoicing; many who were dying of cancer are now well and praying the prayer of faith for the healing of others. Moreover, *"God is no respecter of persons* [does not exhibit partiality, Greek]" (Acts 10:34). The Scriptures say, *"If a man therefore purge himself from these* [iniquities], *he shall be a vessel unto honour, sanctified, and meet for the master's use, and prepared unto every good work"* (2 Tim. 2:21). We cannot be *"prepared unto every good work"* while we are sick in bed. God's new covenant provides that we each will be made *"perfect in every good work to do his will"* (Heb. 13:21). Again, this cannot be while we are sick, and this shows His willingness, in fact, His eagerness, to make us well. He cannot keep His covenant with us without taking away our sicknesses (Exod. 23:25) and fulfilling *"the number of* [our] *days"* (v. 26), according to His promise.

Since it is *"with his stripes we are healed"* (Isa. 53:5), let us not forget what our healing cost; but, with gratitude and love and consecrated service to God, let us stand on His promise and "blow the ram's horn" of faith and thanksgiving until the walls of our affliction fall down flat.

Faith does not wait for the walls to fall down; faith shouts them down!

Six

✦

What Was Paul's "Thorn"?

What Was Paul's "Thorn"?

And lest I should be exalted above measure through the
abundance of the revelations, there was given to me a thorn in the
flesh, the messenger of Satan to buffet me, lest I should be exalted
above measure. For this thing I besought the Lord thrice, that it
might depart from me. And he said unto me, My grace is sufficient
for thee: for my strength is made perfect in weakness. Most gladly
therefore will I rather glory in my infirmities, that the power of
Christ may rest upon me. Therefore I take pleasure in infirmities,
in reproaches, in necessities, in persecutions, in distresses for
Christ's sake: for when I am weak, then am I strong.
—2 Corinthians 12:7–10

One of the most prevalent objections raised today
against the ministry of healing is Paul's *"thorn
in the flesh."* One traditional idea has led to
another. The widespread teaching that God is the
author of disease, and that He has desired that some
of the most devout of His children shall remain sick,
and glorify Him by exhibiting fortitude and patience,
no doubt has led to the idea that Paul had a sickness
that God refused to heal. I do not believe that anyone
who would take time to read all that God has to say on
the subject of healing could ever form such a conclusion.

I am quick to admit that equally devout men may
hold contrary views, not only on this point, but also

on the whole subject of divine healing. It is merely
a matter of study and investigation. Many good men
whose teaching has been that the age of miracles is
past have, while reading the Scriptures, thoughtlessly
passed over the biblical teaching on healing, believing that it is not applicable for our day. Nearly all who
have spoken and written against me have not hesitated to use my name, and to go after me with great
vigor. However, they never have attempted to answer
the scriptural arguments I have presented in my ser-
mons on the subject. I have carefully, without men-
tioning their names, read their statements publicly
and answered them from the Scriptures. If I were
fighting against *flesh and blood*" (Eph. 6:12), I would
name them and go after them "with a vengeance," but
this would not be Christlike. I feel disposed to keep
my hands off God's servants (see 1 Chronicles 16:22;
Psalm 105:15) and to let Him fight my battles for me.

A Clergyman's Absurd Exposition

Before considering the subject of Paul's *"thorn,"* I
quote the following from a transcription of a sermon
preached by a prominent New York clergyman, which
he also revised, printed in great quantities, and dis-
tributed in every home in the vicinity of our revival,
in order to offset our teaching on healing—of which
he had practically no knowledge, having never seen or
heard us. Among other things, he said,

> The fact is—Paul was sick. He was the sickest
> of men. He had one of the worst and most
> painful of oriental diseases. He had ophthal-
> mia—a disease of the eyes. The proof that he
> had it is overwhelming. He tells us he had a

"thorn in the flesh."...When Paul stood before them his eyes filled with unspeakable pus—unspeakable-looking matter running down over his face....Why would they have digged out their eyes for him except that his eyes, as he stood before them, were a pitiable and appealing sight to them—as the eyes of anyone with ophthalmia are? The particular pain of this disease is that it is like a "stake" in the eyes....It is beyond dispute that Paul was a sick man. He says so himself. Paul did not get this disease by infection. How did he get it? Jesus Christ gave it to him. Paul did not want to be sick. He prayed the Lord to heal him from this sickness. He prayed not once, or twice, but three times. He received no answer to his prayers. In spite of all his praying he got no healing. His thrice-offered prayer brought him no cure, not even the hint of healing. That is not all. The Lord said to Paul a very startling thing. He said, *"My grace is sufficient for thee."*...He tells Paul it is better for him to be sick than to be well. He tells Paul it is the divine will that he shall not be cured....He tells Paul divine power can and will operate in and through him better with ophthalmia and sickness than without it....Hear what Paul has to say in response to the Lord concerning his infirmity and the will of the Lord that he shall not be cured of it. These are his words, *"Most gladly therefore will I rather glory in my infirmities, that the power of Christ may rest upon me."* Here is Paul saying just this, "I will glory in my ophthalmia. My eyes may be full of repulsive discharges; I may be the object of pity; no matter, I will glory in it. I will rejoice in my sickness."...In

the quivering flesh and painful suffering of
His apostle, the Lord has written His divine
protest against this unspeakable doctrine, this
brutal transmutation of the cross of Christ into
a center of physical healing.

In answering our brother's arguments on this
point, I will state, first, that the expression "thorn in
the flesh" is only used as an illustration in both the
Old and New Testaments. The symbol of the thorn in
the flesh is not in one single instance in the Bible used
as a symbol of sickness. Every time the expression is
used in the entire Bible, it is specifically stated exactly
what the "thorn in the flesh" is, as we will see. For
instance, in Numbers 33:55, Moses told the children
of Israel, before they entered the land of Canaan,

If ye will not drive out the inhabitants of the
land from before you; then it shall come to pass,
that those which ye let remain of them shall be
pricks in your eyes, and thorns in your sides,
and shall vex you in the land wherein ye dwell.

Here the Scripture itself plainly tells us that the
"pricks in the eyes" and the "thorns in the sides" of
the Israelites were the inhabitants of Canaan, and
not eye trouble or sickness. Some teachers contend
that Paul's *"thorn"* must have been a bodily affliction,
because Paul said that the *"thorn"* was *"in the flesh."* I
answer that, in the case of these Israelites, the Scripture uses the words *"pricks in your **eyes**"* and *"thorns*
*in your **sides**,"* but this does not mean that God was
to stick Canaanites in their eyes and sides. God was
only illustrating, to show that, as a thorn sticking in
the flesh is annoying, so the Canaanites, if allowed

to remain, would be a constant annoyance to the children of Israel.

The Canaanites a Thorn to Israel

Eight years later, Joshua also said, concerning the heathen nations in Canaan, *"They shall be...scourges in your sides, and thorns in your eyes"* (Josh. 23:13). So we see again that the "scourges in their sides and thorns in their eyes" were the Canaanites, and not sore eyes or sore sides. It is plainly stated here, as in all other instances, what the "thorn" was.

Among the last words of David, we read, *"The sons of Belial shall be all of them as thorns"* (2 Sam. 23:6). Without exception, in all these cases, the "thorns" are personalities. As in each of these instances it is definitely stated what the "thorn" was, so Paul definitely stated what his *"thorn"* was. He said it was *"the messenger [angelos, Greek] of Satan"* (2 Cor. 12:7), or, as translated by others, "the angel of the Devil," "Satan's angel," and so forth. This Greek word *angelos* appears 188 times in the Bible, and is translated *"angel"* 181 times and *"messenger"* the other seven times. In all the 188 times in the entire Bible, it is in every case a person and not a thing—without a solitary exception. Hell was made *"for the devil and his angels* [or messengers]" (Matt. 25:41), and an angel or a messenger is always a *person* that one person sends to another, and never a disease.

Paul's Thorn an Angel of Satan

Paul not only tells us that his *"thorn"* was an angel of Satan, but he also tells us what the angel came to do: *"to buffet me,"* or, as Rotherham translates it, *"that **he** might be buffeting me"* (*Emphasized Bible,* emphasis added). Now the word *"buffet"* means "blow after blow," as when waves beat against the boat in which Christ and His disciples were crossing the lake (Mark 4:37), and as when the chief priests and council members buffeted Christ (Matt. 26:67; Mark 14:65). Accordingly, Weymouth translates it, *"Satan's angel to torture me* [dealing blow after blow]." Since buffeting means repeated blows, if Paul's buffeting was disease, it would have had to have been many diseases, or the same disease many times repeated, to be called buffeting. How could the diseases be repeated many times unless he got well in between times?

In speaking of this messenger, or angel, Rotherham's translation uses the pronoun *"he,"* and Weymouth's translation also states, *"Concerning this, three times have I besought the Lord that **he** might leave me"* (emphasis added). Both of these translations use the personal pronoun *he* when speaking of Paul's thorn; so these two pronouns, as well as the word *"angel,"* or *"messenger,"* prove that Paul's thorn was, as he himself plainly showed, a satanic personality and not a disease. We could not use the personal pronoun *he* when speaking of ophthalmia, or any other disease, because there is no gender to ophthalmia. Suppose I were to ask a man how his cancer is; what would you think if you heard him reply, *"He* is a lot worse, and I am suffering terribly." Now, since Paul distinctly stated that his thorn was the angel of Satan sent to buffet him—a demon spirit sent from Satan to make trouble for him wherever he went—why should *we* say it was something else?

Paul's Sufferings

Soon after Paul's conversion, God said to Ananias, *"I will show him how great things he must suffer for my name's sake"* (Acts 9:16)—not by sickness, but by the persecutions that Paul enumerated as his buffetings. Paul had persecuted the Christians from place to place, and now he himself was beginning to experience the same and greater persecutions. Specifying the buffetings instigated by Satan's angel, Paul went on to say, *"Therefore I take pleasure in infirmities, in reproaches, in necessities, in persecutions, in distresses for Christ's sake: for when I am weak, then am I strong."* Paul first mentioned *"infirmities,"* for he realized, and every Christian should realize, his weakness and inability in his own strength to stand up against a satanic messenger, and to pass triumphantly through *"reproaches," "necessities," "persecutions," "distresses,"* and all the other buffetings he elsewhere catalogued. This is why he implored the Lord three times to be rid of "him" (the messenger) who was buffeting him so severely and in so many ways. Christ responded to his thrice-repeated prayer, not by removing the satanic messenger, but by saying, *"My grace* [which is for the "inner" man] *is sufficient for thee: for my strength is made perfect in weakness."*

When Paul saw that the grace of God was sufficient to strengthen him to bear all of these things, he exclaimed, *"Therefore will I rather glory in my infirmities* [weaknesses], *that the power of Christ may rest upon me,...for when I am weak, then am I strong."* How could it be true that Christ's strength was made perfect in Paul's weakness if he was left weak, or unless Paul was an actual partaker of Christ's strength, which would remove the weakness, whether it was physical or spiritual? Without God's strength being imparted to him, is a man powerful when he is weak, either physically or spiritually?

Paul saw that the grace of God that was given to him made his very buffetings, even his imprisonments, work together for his good (Rom. 8:28) and turn out for *"the furtherance of the gospel"* (Phil. 1:12). What servant of God has not learned, and probably more than once, that it is when he is most conscious of his own weakness that the power of Christ rests upon him the most; or that it is when he is consciously weakest in himself that he is the strongest, because he is depending not on his own strength, but on divine strength?

Grace for Spiritual, Not Physical, Infirmities

Paul was clear in teaching that it is the *"life...of Jesus"* that is *"made manifest in our mortal flesh"* (2 Cor. 4:11), but it is nowhere stated in the Scriptures that God gives *grace* to our *bodies*. The very word *grace* shows that it was the "inner man" that needed help, because the grace of God is imparted only to the *"inward man,"* which, Paul said, in his case, was *"renewed day by day"* (v. 16). In other words, grace is for spiritual infirmities, and not for physical ones.

While, in the Old Testament, the terms *"pricks in your eyes, and thorns in your sides"* (Num. 33:55) were used, the Canaanites were not an annoyance to the Israelites in the sense of inflicting any physical disease or infirmities upon their bodies. As the annoying Canaanites were outside the bodies of the Israelites, so Satan's angel was outside of Paul's body; for surely the apostle had no demon inhabiting his body. God's grace and mercy have always been given to enable us to bear our persecutions and temptations, but not to bear our sins and sicknesses, which He bore for us. God has never promised to take away from Christians their *external* buffetings, afflictions, and temptations; He gives us grace to bear them. But, throughout history, He has always been ready to take away the *internal,* or bodily, oppressions of the Devil, as well as our sins.

"For God Was with Him"

Jesus *"went about doing good, and healing all that were oppressed of the devil; for God was with him"* (Acts 10:38). God tells us, *"All that will live godly in Christ Jesus shall suffer persecution"* (2 Tim. 3:12), but He has never said, "They shall remain sick," according to unscriptural views held by many today. This view denies all scriptural precedent. No doubt Paul got the expression *"thorn in the flesh"* from reading the Old Testament Scriptures; and because the term illustrated their external and not their bodily annoyances, he used the expression to illustrate his own buffetings.

If the *"infirmities* [weaknesses]" of which Paul spoke in our text passage were physical, and, according to the above-quoted writer, Paul was "the sickest of men," and God would not remove the thorn by giving him strength, how could he labor *"more abundantly than they all"* (1 Cor. 15:10)? If the sickest of men can accomplish more work than a well man, then let us all pray for sickness in order that we also may do more work for God.

After realizing that God's strength was *"made perfect in* [his] *weakness,"* Paul could take pleasure not only in his *"infirmities,"* but also in the buffetings that he mentioned: *"reproaches," "necessities," "persecutions,"* and *"distresses."* Note that, among other things, Paul mentioned *"necessities,"* meaning his financial buffetings, which he also referred to in his first letter to the Corinthians written a year before. He said, *"Even unto this present hour we both hunger, and thirst, and are naked, and are buffeted, and have no certain dwellingplace"* (1 Cor. 4:11), showing that Paul's idea of buffetings was not a permanent sickness.

Paul Enumerated His Buffetings

If Paul's thorn was ophthalmia, or sore eyes, which he did not mention in this passage, instead of these reproaches and so forth, which he *did* mention, why did he not say he took pleasure in the former instead of in the latter? Not only here, but elsewhere in his second letter to the Corinthians, Paul enumerated in detail his buffetings instigated by Satan's angel. In addition to the reproaches, necessities, persecutions, and distresses mentioned in our text, in the sixth chapter he mentioned *"stripes," "imprisonments," "tumults," "labours," "watchings," "fastings"* (v. 5), *"dishonour," "evil report," "deceivers"* (v. 8), *"as dying, and, behold, we live; as chastened, and not killed; as sorrowful, yet alway rejoicing; as poor, yet making many rich; as having nothing, and yet possessing all things"* (vv. 9–10); and in the eleventh chapter,

> *stripes above measure, in prisons more frequent, in deaths oft. Of the Jews five times received I forty stripes save one. Thrice was I beaten with rods, once was I stoned, thrice I suffered shipwreck, a night and a day I have been in the deep; in journeyings often, in perils of waters, in perils of robbers, in perils by mine own countrymen, in perils by the heathen, in perils in the*

city, in perils in the wilderness, in perils in the sea, in perils among false brethren; in weariness and painfulness, in watchings often, in hunger and thirst, in fastings often, in cold and nakedness. (2 Cor. 11:23–27)

In 1 Corinthians 4, Paul also mentioned that he was *"reviled," "persecuted"* (v. 12), *"defamed," "made as the filfth of the world,…the offscouring of all things unto this day"* (v. 13).

Questions Worth Considering

Who but Satan's angel could be responsible for all these sufferings? In enumerating them, we see that Paul mentioned almost everything that one could think of *except* sickness, or ophthalmia. The one thing that he did not mention, and which is conspicuous for its absence, tradition seizes upon and says was his thorn. Why do these opposers substitute "sore eyes" or "sickness," neither of which Paul mentioned, for all of these buffetings that he *did* mention?

Although it is believed by many good men, one writer remarked that this widespread perversion of the Scriptures dealing with Paul's thorn in the flesh is certainly inspired by Satan, because it gives him the privilege of carrying on his evil work of afflicting and tormenting the bodies of humanity.

Since healing is an essential element of the Gospel, how could Paul enjoy *"the fulness of the blessing of the gospel"* (Rom. 15:29), as he did, and remain sick? Is healing not a part of the blessing of the Gospel? Even such conservative scholars as those constituting the Episcopalian Commission on Healing agree that "the healing of the body is an essential element of the Gospel."

Suppose our brother is correct in stating that Paul was the "sickest of men," suffering with ophthalmia. Is it not strange that when the Ephesians saw the pus running from Paul's eyes and found that God would not heal him, this sight gave them faith for *"special miracles"* to be worked in their behalf? For it is stated in the Scriptures that

> *God wrought special miracles by the hands of Paul: so that from his body were brought unto the sick handkerchiefs or aprons, and the diseases departed from them, and the evil spirits went out of them.*   *(Acts 19:11–12)*

The Scriptures never speak of special miracles in connection with any but this "sickest" apostle. Today, if handkerchiefs were brought from one suffering with ophthalmia, rather than laying them on the sick for healing, we would burn them to keep from spreading the infection.

The Case of the Cripple at Lystra

Is it not also strange that when the heathen cripple at Lystra heard Paul preach *"the gospel"* (Acts 14:7) and got a glimpse of Paul's eyes with their "repulsive discharges," the sight at once gave him faith to walk for the first time in his life, and Paul *"perceiving that he had faith to be healed, said with a loud voice, Stand upright on thy feet. And he leaped and walked"* (vv. 9–10)? This heathen cripple had never witnessed a miracle or ever heard the Gospel preached until he heard it from "the sickest of men" whom God willed "shall not be cured."

WHAT WAS PAUL'S "THORN"? ✦

Again, is it not marvelous how Paul, with "unspeakable pus—unspeakable-looking matter running down over his face," "the sickest of men," suffering with the "worst and most painful of oriental diseases," "a pitiable and appealing sight to them," and when "Jesus Christ gave it to him," telling him "it is the divine will that he shall not be cured"—I repeat, is it not marvelous how Paul in this condition could *"make the **Gentiles** obedient, by word and deed, **through mighty signs and wonders**, by the power of the Spirit of God,...from Jerusalem, and round about unto Illyricum"* (Rom. 15:18–19, emphasis added)?

In addition, on the island of Melita, after seeing Paul's unsightly disease, which had to have remained because "divine power can and will operate in and through him better with ophthalmia and sickness than without it," first the father of Publius, and then *"all the other sick people in the island came and were cured"* (Acts 28:9 WEYMOUTH).

Do the Sick Glory in Sickness?

The brother quoted at the beginning of this chapter said,

> Here is Paul saying just this, "I will glory in my ophthalmia. My eyes may be full of repulsive discharges; I may be the object of pity; no matter, I will glory in it. I will rejoice in my sickness."

Since men such as this teach that it was right for Paul to glory in his being "the sickest of men," why do they not also glory in *their* sicknesses, instead of doing their best to be rid of them? If they glory in their "thorns," why have some of them gone to surgeons to have them cut out?

Some teachers hold that Paul's thorn was a partial blindness, caused by the brightness of the divine light that shone upon him at his conversion. He himself told us, in the year A.D. 60, when he wrote 2 Corinthians, that it was *"above fourteen years ago"* (2 Cor. 12:2) that he received the abundance of the revelations (vv. 2–4) that occasioned the giving of the *"thorn in the flesh"* (v. 7). That would make it twelve years after his conversion that the thorn was given, this epistle having been written twenty-six years after his conversion. Moreover, it would be almost blasphemy to speak of a partial blindness caused by a personal glimpse of the glorified Christ as *"the messenger of Satan."*

Why Paul's "Thorn"?

Paul distinctly stated that his buffeting by the messenger was given him *"lest* [he] *should be exalted above measure through the abundance of the revelations."* Is it because of the abundance of their revelations that the sick everywhere today must be taught to regard their sickness as a "thorn," which must remain, lest *they* be exalted?

Since Paul's thorn was no hindrance to his faith for the healing of *"all the other sick people in the island"* (Acts 28:9 WEYMOUTH) of Melita and elsewhere, why should it hinder ours; or why should it be taught today everywhere as a hindrance to what little faith for healing the sick may have received? The Bible says that *"faith cometh by hearing"* (Rom. 10:17), but in these days, faith "leaveth by hearing"—hearing these foolish doctrines. The widespread error concerning Paul's thorn in the flesh severs the Gospel, and entirely removes the foundation upon which faith for healing must rest—unless the sick one receives, from the Spirit and not from the Bible, a special revelation that he is to be healed.

I have noticed from the writings of teachers who deny divine healing that they are quick to mention the slightest physical defect in those who teach healing and are seeing the sick healed; yet they argue that it was proper for Paul, who is the most outstanding New Testament teacher of healing, to have, as they contend, the "thorn" of bodily affliction. If we could duplicate Paul's wonderful ministry of healing while "unspeakable pus" was all the time running from *our* eyes, would not this be seized upon by these very teachers as a ground for ridicule?

Paul's Thorn Not a Hindrance to Labor in the Lord

The Scriptures show that Paul's thorn did not hinder him from laboring *"more abundantly"* than all others (1 Cor. 15:10); but those who are taught that their sickness is a "thorn" that must remain are often incapacitated by *their* "thorn" from any labor, not even being able to care for themselves, but increasing other people's labors by having to be waited upon. It was the apostle Paul who wrote that we may be *"prepared unto every good work"* (2 Tim. 2:21), *"thoroughly furnished unto all good works"* (2 Tim. 3:17), *"zealous of good works"* (Titus 2:14), *"careful to maintain good works"* (Titus 3:8), and *"perfect in every good work to do his will"* (Heb. 13:21). How can the multitude of Christians confined to their sickrooms by a "thorn in the flesh" *"abound to every good work"* (2 Cor. 9:8)? Do these several Scriptures belong only to well Christians?

If Christ's words, *"My grace is sufficient,"* mean that He was telling Paul to remain sick, it would be the first and only instance in the Bible in which God ever told anyone to keep his disease; and then the very fact of its being a solitary exception would prove the rule, and what the Scriptures abundantly show, that He healed all others. Why do so many of these teachers today reverse the Scriptures and make Paul's thorn the prominent point when discussing healing, and keep in the background the universal policy of healing revealed throughout the history recorded in the Bible? Paul's thorn did not hinder him from finishing his course for God (2 Tim. 4:7), while present-day teaching concerning Paul's thorn has sent multitudes, often after many years of terrible suffering, to premature graves, with their course only half run—a constantly recurring and horrible tragedy!

Paul's Praying a Worthy Example

If the physically afflicted who believe this latter-day teaching will follow Paul by praying until God speaks to them and tells them, as they think He did Paul, that He wants them to keep their afflictions, and gives them the reason for it, we would quickly say, "Amen!" for we love the will of God.

In Galatians 4:13, Paul did say, *"Ye know how through infirmity of the flesh I preached the gospel unto you at the first."* Probably the infirmity here was physical, but *"at the first"* does not mean that he remained weak. Does it not mean the opposite? Or else why would he say *"at the first"*? Probably, as some scholars believe, this was just after his stoning at Lystra.

After Paul, in the plainest words, has told us what his thorn was, how strange that ministers today should say it is something else, and use it against the scriptural doctrine of healing, when Paul himself was the greatest teacher on this subject among the apostles and other writers of the New Testament.

Paul's Preaching Stimulates Faith

For instance, it was the gospel Paul preached in Ephesus that gave faith for the *"special miracles"* (Acts 19:11) of healing mentioned earlier. He said, concerning his own preaching there, *"I kept back nothing that was profitable unto you"* (Acts 20:20). If all preachers today would keep back nothing that was profitable, they would surely all be teaching healing.

In Romans 15:18–19, it was Paul who said he *"fully preached the gospel of Christ* [preached the full Gospel],*"* and made *"the Gentiles obedient, by word and deed, through mighty signs and wonders, by the power of the Spirit of God,…from Jerusalem, and round about unto Illyricum."*

Twenty-five years after he had become an apostle, he wrote to the Corinthians, *"For this cause many are weak and sickly among you"* (1 Cor. 11:30). If Paul's thorn was physical infirmity, or he was sick, they would probably have written back to him, asking, "For what cause are *you* weak and sickly?"

It was Paul who wrote: *"Know ye not that your body is the temple of the Holy Ghost?"* (1 Cor. 6:19). *"Know ye not that your bodies are the members of Christ?"* (v. 15). *"We are members of his body, of his flesh, and of his bones"* (Eph. 5:30). *"We have 'the firstfruits of the Spirit* [firstfruits of our spiritual and physical salvation]'"* (Rom. 8:23). *"That the life also of Jesus might be made manifest in our mortal flesh"* (2 Cor. 4:11). *"The Spirit…shall also quicken your mortal* [not dead] *bodies"* (Rom. 8:11). *"[Christ] is the saviour of the body"* (Eph. 5:23). *"The body is...for the Lord; and the Lord* [is] *for the body"* (1 Cor. 6:13).

Called to Be Saints

Paul is the apostle who wrote:

Unto the church of God which is at Corinth,... called to be saints, with all that in every place call upon the name of Jesus Christ our Lord....God hath set...in the church...miracles, then gifts of healings.   *(1 Cor. 1:2, 12:28)*

The gifts and calling of God are without repentance [are not revoked].   *(Rom. 11:29)*

He also wrote that all are commanded to *"covet earnestly the best gifts"* (1 Cor. 12:31). Paul did not believe, as men are teaching today, that these blessings were confined to Israel, but he believed that the *"middle wall of partition"* had been *"broken down"* (Eph. 2:14), that in Christ there is *"neither Jew nor Greek"* (Gal. 3:28), and that we are *"all one in Christ Jesus"* (v. 28). Accordingly, he healed the Gentile at Lystra who had been crippled from birth, the same as Peter and John did for the Jewish cripple at the Beautiful Gate. (See Acts 3:2–8.) Paul also believed that the Old Testament types were *"written for our admonition"* (1 Cor. 10:11), that *"they which are of faith, the same are the children of Abraham"* (Gal. 3:7), that *"to Abraham and his seed were the promises made"* (v. 16), and that *"if ye be Christ's, then are ye Abraham's seed, and heirs according to the promise"* (v. 29).

WHAT WAS PAUL'S "THORN"? ✦

Paul on the Island of Melita

It was Paul who taught that it is *"in him* [Christ]" that *"all the promises of God...are yea, and...Amen, unto the glory of God by us* [Gentiles]" (2 Cor. 1:20). In other words, that all the promises of God, including all His promises to heal, owe their existence and power to the substitutionary work of Christ for us; that the redeeming work of Christ was for *all*. Accordingly, the very last chapter of Acts shows us that Paul believed and proved that it was God's will to heal, not just some, but *"all the other sick people in the island"* of Melita (Acts 28:9 WEYMOUTH).

Paul differentiated between miracles and healing, and therefore he did not believe that *every* person would instantly be made whole. We know this because he left Trophimus sick at Miletum (2 Tim. 4:20), and Epaphroditus was *"sick nigh unto death"* (Phil. 2:27) for the Gospel's sake (or from overwork), and he did not recover instantaneously (vv. 25–30). Paul was not a fanatic concerning the natural laws of health, which are as divine as God's miracles, and he did not hesitate to recommend "the fruit of the vine" in place of only water for Timothy's stomach trouble (1 Tim. 5:23).

Paul believed in the sick themselves having faith for healing, for he did not say to the cripple, *"Stand upright on thy feet"* (Acts 14:10) until he perceived that *"he had faith to be healed"* (v. 9). Jesus Himself could do no miracle in Nazareth because of community unbelief. (See Mark 6:1–6.)

An Instructive Résumé

Is it not strange how any minister can set aside the whole Bible, as far as the subject of healing is concerned, keeping in the background:

- God's redemptive and covenant name, JEHOVAH-RAPHA
- God's covenant of healing
- The teaching and promises of healing in the Old Testament types
- The universal precedent of healing set throughout the history of the Old Testament
- The words, teaching, commands, promises, and healing ministry of Christ, by which He revealed the will of God for our bodies
- The gifts of healing established in the church
- The church ordinance of anointing, which is commanded
- The fact that Christ bore our sicknesses as well as our sins on Calvary
- The multiplied thousands of those who have been healed since the days of the apostles, down to and including our days in particular

Is it not strange that ministers can set all of this aside, and, when speaking on the subject of healing, choose as their text the Scripture concerning Paul's *"thorn,"* which scholars admit they cannot prove has any reference to either sickness or healing?

Seven

✦

Thirty-One Questions
to Consider

Seven

✦

Thirty-One Questions To Consider[*]

To summarize and review many of the main points from the previous chapters regarding healing in the Atonement, here are thirty-one questions for your consideration:

1. Since the seven compound names of Jehovah—one of which is JEHOVAH-RAPHA [*"I am the LORD that healeth thee"* (Exod. 15:26)]—reveal His redemptive relationship toward each person, do they not point to Calvary?

2. Since all the promises of God are *"yea"* and *"Amen"* in Him (2 Cor. 1:20), do these seven names, including JEHOVAH-RAPHA (The Lord Our Healer), not owe their existence and their power to the redeeming work of Christ on the cross?

3. Does every believer not have the same redemptive right to call upon Christ as JEHOVAH-RAPHA (the Healer of his body) as he has to call upon Him as JEHOVAH-TSIDKENU (the Healer of his soul)? Is His

* These questions were originally offered for consideration by the author when he preached at the Alliance Tabernacle in Toronto, Canada.

151

name not given for healing inasmuch as it is for salvation?

4. If bodily healing is to be obtained independently of Calvary, as opposers teach, why was it that no blessing of the Year of Jubilee was to be announced by the sounding of the trumpet until the Day of Atonement?

5. If healing for the body was not a part of Christ's redeeming work, why were types of the Atonement given in connection with healing throughout the Old Testament?

6. If healing was not in the Atonement, why were the dying Israelites required to look at the type of the Atonement for bodily healing? If both forgiveness and healing came by a look at the type, why not from the Antitype?

7. Since the Israelites' curse was removed by the lifting up of the type of Christ, was our curse not a disease also removed by the lifting up of Christ Himself? (See Galatians 3:13.)

8. In the passage, *"Surely he hath borne our griefs* [sicknesses], *and carried our sorrows* [pains]" (Isa. 53:4), why are the same Hebrew verbs for *"borne"* and *"carried"* employed as are used in verses eleven and twelve for the substitutionary bearing of sin unless they have the same substitutionary and expiatory character?

9. If healing was not provided for everyone in redemption, how did the multitudes obtain from Christ what God did not provide?

10. If the body was not included in redemption, how can there be a resurrection, or how can corruption put on incorruption, or mortality put on immortality (1 Cor. 15:53)? Were the physical as well as the spiritual earnests (foretastes) of our coming redemption not enjoyed by God's people throughout history?

11. Why should the Second Adam not take away all that the first Adam brought upon us?

12. Since the church is the body of Christ, does God want the body of Christ sick? Is it not His will to heal any part of the body of Christ? If not, why does He command anyone who is sick in the body of Christ to be anointed for healing (James 5:14)?

13. Are human imperfections of any sort, whether they are physical or moral, God's will, or are they man's mistakes?

14. Since *"the body is...for the Lord"* (1 Cor. 6:13), *"a living sacrifice...unto God"* (Rom. 12:1), would He not rather have a well body than a wrecked one? If not, how can He make us *"perfect in every good work to do his will"* (Heb. 13:21) or have us *"thoroughly furnished unto all good works"* (2 Tim. 3:17)?

15. Since bodily healing in the New Testament was called a mercy (see, for example, Philippians 2:27), and it was mercy and compassion that moved Jesus to heal all who came to Him (see, for example, Matthew 9:36), is the promise of God not still true, that He is *"plenteous in mercy unto all them that call upon* [Him]*"* (Ps. 86:5)?

16. Does the glorious Gospel dispensation not offer as much mercy and compassion to its sufferers as did the darker dispensations? If not, why would God withdraw this mercy and this Old Testament privilege from a better dispensation with its *"better covenant"* (Heb. 8:6)?

17. If, as some teach, God has another method for our healing today, why would God adopt a less successful method for our better dispensation?

18. Since Christ came to do the Father's will, was the universal healing of all the sick who came to Him not a revelation of the will of God for our bodies?

19. Did Jesus not emphatically say that He would continue His same works in answer to our prayers while He is with the Father (John 14:12–14), and is this promise alone not a complete answer to all opposers?

20. Why would the Holy Spirit, who healed all the sick before His dispensation began, do less after He entered into office on the Day of Pentecost? Or did the Miracle Worker enter office to do away with miracles?

21. Is the book of the Acts of the Holy Spirit not a revelation of the way He wants to continue to act through the church?

22. How can God justify us and at the same time require us to remain under the curse of the law that Jesus redeemed us from by bearing it for us on the cross? (See Galatians 3:13.)

23. Since *"the Son of God was manifested, that he might destroy the works of the devil"* (1 John 3:8), has He now relinquished this purpose that He retained even during the bloody sweat of Gethsemane and the tortures of Calvary? Or does He now want the works of the Devil in our bodies to continue what He formerly wanted to destroy? Does God want a cancer, a *"plague"* (Deut. 28:61), *"the curse of the law"* (Gal. 3:13), *"the works of the devil"* in the members of Christ? *"Know ye not that your bodies are the members of Christ?"* (1 Cor. 6:15).

24. Are the proofs of divine healing among the 184 people who testified in this Tabernacle the last two Friday nights less bright and convincing than the proofs of spiritual redemption among professed Christians today?

    Are these 184 who have been healed not in better health physically than a similar number of professing Christians are spiritually?

    Would the physical health of these 184 not compare favorably with the spiritual health of even the same number of ministers of our day?

25. Would the argument commonly employed against divine healing, drawn from its failures, if employed against justification, regeneration, and all the rest, not be simply overwhelming?

26. Does the fact that Christ could do no miracle at Nazareth (Mark 6:1–6) prove anything except the unbelief of the people; or would it be right to conclude, because of the failure of Christ's disciples to

cast out the epileptic spirit from the boy, that it was not God's will to deliver him (Matt. 17:14–21)? Christ proved by healing him that it is God's will to heal even those who fail to receive healing.

27. Is God not as willing to show the mercy of healing to His worshippers as He is to show the mercy of forgiveness to His enemies (Rom. 5:10; 8:32)?

28. If Paul (as a New York minister has said) "was the sickest of men," suffering from the eye inflammation ophthalmia, or if, as others teach, his *"thorn in the flesh"* (2 Cor. 12:7) was physical weakness instead of what Paul himself said it was, *"the messenger [angelos, Greek] of Satan"* (v. 7), or "Satan's angel," inflicting the many buffetings that Paul enumerated, how could he labor *"more abundantly"* (1 Cor. 15:10) than all the other apostles? Or since he had strength to do more work than all the others, how could his "weaknesses" be physical? Since Paul's *"thorn"* did not hinder His faith for the universal healing of all *"the rest of the sick folk in the island* [of Melita]" (Acts 28:9 MOFFATT), why should it hinder ours? Would Paul's failure to be healed, if he was sick, not have hindered the universal faith of these heathen for their healing? Why do traditional teachers substitute "ophthalmia" or "sickness" (neither of which Paul mentioned) for the *"reproaches,"* *"necessities,"* *"persecutions,"* *"distresses"* (2 Cor. 12:10), and all the other buffetings at the hands of "Satan's angel" that he *did* mention? If the former constitute his *"thorn,"* why did he not say he took pleasure in the former instead of the latter? How could Paul, sick in body, or with the

unsightly disease ophthalmia, and unable to be healed, *"make the Gentiles obedient, by word and deed, **through mighty signs and wonders**"* (Rom. 15:18–19, emphasis added)?

29. If sickness is the will of God, then would not every physician be a lawbreaker, every trained nurse be defying the Almighty, every hospital be a house of rebellion instead of a house of mercy; and instead of supporting hospitals, should we not then do our utmost to close them?

30. Since Jesus in the Gospels never commissioned anybody to preach the Gospel without commanding him to heal the sick, how can we obey this command if there is no Gospel ("good news") of healing to proclaim to the sick as a basis for their faith? Or since faith is expecting God to keep His promise, how can there be faith for healing if God has not promised it? And since the Bible is full of promises of healing, are they not all Gospel ("good news") to the sick? Since *"faith cometh by hear-ing...the word"* (Rom. 10:17), how can the sick have faith for healing if there is nothing for them to hear?

31. "Could the loving heart of the Son of God, who had compassion upon the sick, and healed all who had need of healing, cease to regard the sufferings of His own when He had become exalted at the right hand of the Father?"

—Kenneth Mackenzie

Eight

✦

Testimonies of Healing

Eight

✦

Testimonies of Healing

Miraculous Healing of One Leads Many to Salvation—Physical Blessings Also Follow

The testimonies combined under the first heading call attention to the spiritual and physical blessings that constantly follow the healing of a single individual. We see this precedent in the Scriptures. The result of the healing of Aeneas was that all Lydda and Saron turned to God (Acts 9:32–35). His healing was as important as the salvation of two cities. Through the healing of the lame man at the Beautiful gate of the temple, 5,000 men were saved (Acts 3:1–4:4). Paul told us of God's purpose *"to make the Gentiles obedient, by word and deed, through mighty signs and wonders, by the power of the Spirit of God"* (Rom. 15:18–19).

People who are healed constantly receive with their physical blessings an infilling of the Spirit and a compassion that sends them out to seek the salvation of others and to tell them that they, too, can receive from a loving God the healing that they need for their own bodies.

Thrilling testimonies telling of such a "chain of blessings" are continually being received.

Saved and healed of her affliction, Mrs. J. B. Long of Pittsburgh, Pennsylvania, sought to fulfill the

promise she made to take a message of divine healing to some sick friends. Prompted by the Holy Spirit,
she went to the altar with her own bodily affliction.
Anointed by the Reverend E. D. Whiteside and evangelist Fred Francis Bosworth, she arose to be a spiritual blessing to others. How faithfully she is fulfilling
her promise is shown in her determination to carry
the Gospel with its messages of bodily healing to the
sick in soul and body. Souls saved and bodies healed
bring blessed assurance of happiness to the ignorant
and forsaken.

Cracked Knees—Painful to Walk—
Now Climb Steps

More than a year ago, I was healed of total
deafness in my right ear and also cracked knee-
caps. The deafness was due to a nervous breakdown that I had more than ten years ago, and
it left me deaf for more than five years. On my
way to church one night in company with Miss
Elizabeth Taylor, I fell and cracked my knees.
They caused me great suffering for several
years and kept growing worse all the time.

I could scarcely go up and down the steps,
but now, praise God, I can run. I live on the
hilltop, and to take the streetcar, it is necessary to go down a flight of 185 steps. I used to
suffer agony in holding onto the rail and trying
to get down, but bless His dear name, I can
now run down, and I never go down those steps
without lifting my heart to God in true thank-
fulness for what He has done.

It was during the first Bosworth campaign
in Pittsburgh that I was healed. I sat in the
meeting looking at the wonderful sight of people

being saved and healed. I had been saved thirty-eight years before when I was just a little girl. The thought came to me that night how sweet it would be to be able to take a message of divine healing to some of my sick friends. Just then the thought came to me, How can I carry the gospel of healing to anyone unless I have a testimony of my own? That decided me.

Without the least hesitation, I went to the altar with my own bodily ills, and was anointed. Brother F. F. Bosworth and the Reverend E. D. Whiteside prayed with me, and I was instantly healed. It was complete, and during the year following my healing, I have never had any return of the trouble. I was saved to serve and I was anxious to be healed so that I might serve Him better. As I walked up Ohio Street that night to take the car, I suddenly seemed to be in a new world.

I believe at that time God gave me a fresh baptism of His Holy Spirit. This has been the most wonderful year of my life, for God has so sweetly used me in His service. Truly, there is joy in the service of the King. I have had more spiritual blessings follow my healing and Christ has been nearer and dearer to me than ever before.

I find the great secret of this joy comes from testifying to the power of God. The night I was healed, I testified to a member of my church on the car. I knew it would spread. The following week, my pastor called me aside, told me what he had heard, and asked if it was true. I told him it was true. He could not see it my way at first, but when I gave him Scripture for it (Matt. 8:16–17), the Lord fully convinced him.

The following week, our services opened. It was the best revival we ever knew. One evening each week, our pastor spoke on divine healing. The invitation went out to those seeking salvation or healing. The pastor anointed, while Brother I. E. Hoover and I laid hands on the sick. Many were healed while we prayed with them.

I felt I was just an empty vessel lying at the Master's feet, ready to be filled and used in His service. The next day after my healing, I asked the Lord to send me to someone who needed healing, that I might tell my story. The face of a friend of mine came before me, Mrs. Sadie Robinson. I went to call and found her in bed, having been ill for many weeks.

The next day, Brother I. E. Hoover offered his vehicle; we took her to the Christian and Missionary Alliance Tabernacle, Arch Street, where she was anointed by Brother Bosworth and healed. It resulted in the salvation of four in her family. God has been wonderfully using her, to His honor and glory. One of her neighbors, Mrs. Bigley, a great sufferer for thirty years, whose testimony follows, had heard of Mrs. Robinson's healing and sent for her and myself. We spent an afternoon with her studying the Bible together. She was very anxious.

I went again in a few days with Mr. Fred Collins who was healed at the Bosworth meeting, Mr. I. E. Hoover, and the Reverend Kreamer, the Baptist minister. We prayed with Mrs. Bigley, anointed her, and she was healed.

That was on Saturday. The following Tuesday, she was up, perfectly well, had on her shoes, and without a sign of her old trouble.

She was beaming with happiness, and has had no return of any of her troubles, which had been of thirty years' duration. Her son was also brought to Christ and healed at the Sheraden Tabernacle.

I find that the most important thing in the Christian life is perfect obedience to the will of God. It is very sweet to live in the inner circle. Although it may cut us off from those around us, yet it is sweet to know we have His approval.

Mrs. J. B. Long, Pittsburgh, PA
December 29, 1921

Miss Taylor Confirms Mrs. Long's Testimony

I am well acquainted with Mrs. Long. We both belong to the same church, and I was with her the night she fell and cracked her knee-caps. She was laid up for some time. They were also healed, and she has no more trouble with them.

Elizabeth Taylor, Pittsburgh, PA
December 29, 1921

Healing of Nervous Breakdown Results in Salvation of Husband and Three Daughters

In the early fall of last year, 1920, I was taken very ill with a nervous breakdown of body and mind, as well as inward trouble. I was kept at home for two weeks under the care of one of our best doctors. One day I would seemingly be better, but the next day would be worse, and so on until some kind friends came and took me to their home in the country. There I was free from all city noise and I received the best treatment and all the love and kindness that one could receive. I was there six weeks, but had just the same results, being kept under a quieting tonic most of the time, nights as well as days. After six weeks, I was brought back, if anything, worse than before. The day after being brought home, the blessed Lord sent one of His faithful servants to me, Mrs. Mary Long. She gave me her testimony and prayed for me. She was all love and kindness. One day she mended some of my son's greasy working clothes, and another day helped the children prepare the meal. I tell this to the glory of God to show what one will do when the Holy Spirit has the right of way with them. On Monday, November 15, 1920, she and two others, dear Christians, came with an automobile and took me to the Tabernacle on Arch Street. There Brother Bosworth prayed for me and anointed me, and I was healed immediately. Bless God, Jesus did it in answer to prayer. It took three to help me into the Tabernacle, but I walked out without the aid of a human hand, leaning heavily on the arm of Jesus.

Oh, He was and still is so precious to me. The morning of the fifteenth, the day I was taken to the Tabernacle, my husband and family truly believed I could not possibly live out the day. That evening, I prepared the evening meal with very little help from the children. My healing has been the means of my husband and three daughters giving their hearts to Christ. They are standing firmly today on the solid Rock, Christ Jesus, praise God.

The next morning, the sixteenth, I took a streetcar and went to the meeting without a human being with me. Jesus was with me and still is. The day after that, the seventeenth, I cleaned three rooms completely, singing and praising God all the time. Since then, I have been attacked a few times, and each time the dear Lord has sent Sister Long to me, and she has prayed for me; and bless God, each time I have been healed. I truly have much to praise God for.

I knew Sister Long before her healing, how she was afflicted, and since she has been delivered. I praise God for the way He is using her to His glory. May He add His blessing to my testimony.

Your sister in the Lord Jesus Christ,
Mrs. Sadie Robinson, Pittsburgh, PA
December 31, 1921

Nervousness Cured: Suffered for Years

I have suffered from a nervous condition for five years. It arose from spinal trouble, the doctors said. I had no control over the muscles in my head. My face and mouth were constantly twitching and distorted. My eyes were similarly affected. My head moved about. Specialist after specialist was consulted. None of them were able to help me. They could not determine what caused the trouble. Finally, I heard of the meetings at the Sheraden Tabernacle. I came on November 4. When the invitation was given, I went forward and was prayed for and anointed. The twitching and contortions stopped immediately and have not returned.

Miss Hazel D. Benz, Crafton, PA

In a letter written several months later, confirming her testimony, Miss Benz said,

Since I was healed of my serious nervous trouble four months ago, my mother, sister, brother-in-law, and stepfather have been saved. I have myself gained eighteen and one-half pounds in weight.

Varicose Veins—Blood Pressure—Limbs Swelled— Trouble Gone

In commemoration of the birth of our Lord and Savior Jesus Christ on this beautiful Christmas Day, I know of no better tribute than the testimony of my dear mother and myself. I hope that, in giving it, it may be used to bring peace and joy to some poor, tired sinner or to help some poor sufferer to be healed, all "to the glory of God."

About five months ago, my mother, who had been troubled with varicose veins for over thirty years, along with an awful high blood pressure and swelling of the limbs developing into a dropsical condition for nearly ten years, and who had been unable to walk for ten weeks, heard of one of our neighbors, Mrs. Robinson, being healed by "faith in God." The case was so wonderful that we inquired and found out that a Mrs. J. B. Long had taken this woman to some church; so we found where Mrs. Long lived and asked her to come and see Mother. Mrs. Robinson and Mrs. Long came and prayed with Mother and explained the wonderful things in store for all who believed. Later, Mrs. Long and three members of the church came to see us, prayed with Mother, and anointed her. Three days later, she could put her shoes on and walk, which she had not done for ten long weeks.

Meanwhile, Mother had read her Bible, and as God revealed Himself to her in prayer, she was greatly blessed, and all the pain and aches left her limbs, the varicose veins started to dry up, and all swelling to recede. Her general health became better and the high blood pressure began to disappear, something that the doctors had claimed was impossible except by electric treatments. They had advised her removal to a hospital months ago.

Today finds Mother in better health than she has been in years, and there has been no return of any of her old ailments. Glory to God for His blessings. Being saved and healed herself, she has found consolation and happiness in the work of God and in His promises.

Meanwhile, Mrs. Long continued to call on us. She was never in a hurry to go and always had prayer before leaving.

When I saw the wonderful works of God in my mother, I, too, started to search the Scriptures and found God's promises were the same to me if I believed. On one of Mrs. Long's visits, she told me of her own life and of others. After telling me it was the last day of the Tabernacle services, she persuaded me to go. Well, with Mrs. Robinson and her husband, who had also been saved and healed, I went. It was a day I will never forget as long as I live.

I listened to the evangelist, and at the end of his sermon, he called for all who wished to be saved or healed or prayed for to come forward. All the time I had been listening, I had been silently praying for God to lead me. With Brother Robinson, I went forward and I was saved by the blood of Christ.

I had been suffering from nervous disorders and bad health for fifteen years, had been through three very serious operations, and never had a well day. After being prayed for and anointed by one of the workers, I came home and, glory to God, "by His stripes" I was healed. I have enjoyed my meals ever since, have never been bothered with any stomach trouble at all, and my nerves have been strengthened wonderfully. Mother and I are so happy, and the further on we go, the sweeter this life gets. It seems we both are getting the good things God has in store for all who believe. I also want to mention this: in one week I prayed to God for five things that a person would think were nearly impossible; but glory be to His holy name, I got all I asked for.

Please print this so that someone may see it and profit by our experience and get peace and happiness like we did. All who believe on the Lord Jesus Christ will be saved. This is His promise, and praise His blessed name, He never breaks His promises. Our Bible is a great source of happiness now, and my one hope is that God may use me in the advancement of His work in any way He chooses. We are thankful to God and will always be His coworkers here until He takes us to be with Him over there.

Carson A. Bigley, Pittsburgh, PA
December 25, 1917

Eye Specialists Outrivaled by Simple Faith

I was a church member and had been one for five years. I knew that Jesus was the Son of God and that He shed His blood on the cross. But I did not know—had never heard that it was for me—that I was lost and that I could be saved and know it, instead of waiting until I died to learn whether I got to heaven or not.

However, I was proud of the church and would never think of going into another denomination's meeting. But I was in need of healing. I had been very farsighted all my life and had been cross-eyed in one eye for fifteen years. I wore powerful glasses for over eleven years and had to have them changed by a specialist about every six months. When deprived of my glasses for just a few moments, I would suffer severe headaches, and could not see well enough to distinguish faces or furniture. Everything would be hazy and blurred.

A friend in Pittsburgh sent me a *Tribune* giving testimonies and announcing the Bosworth meetings in Detroit. I went to the meeting January 11, 1921, and was saved right in my seat. I don't remember the text or anything about that night except that I felt much lighter when I went out than when I came in. That week, the Lord began dealing with me, and "behold old things passed away and all things became as new."

The next morning, I went up for healing. Brother B. B. Bosworth prayed for me, and I was instantly healed. He held up the seeker's card and I could read everything on it. I was just dumbfounded. For two hours, my eyes were perfectly straight and my vision normal. Then, both went back and were worse than they had ever been all the rest of that day and all the next day.

Some of the folks at home tried to urge me to put my glasses back on—they said that I would go blind altogether. But, thank God, I refused and just trusted Him. The following day, my eyes were perfectly straight and kept getting stronger all along, until now they are just as normal as anyone's. I forgot to mention that during the time the Lord was testing me, I could read my Bible, but nothing else. Two weeks after the Lord so wonderfully healed me, He baptized and filled me with the Holy Spirit and still keeps me filled. I do praise God that He put healing in the Gospel and that the Bosworth brothers ever came to Detroit and told us about it. Since the Lord healed me, I have never even had a headache from my eyes.

There is no one more real to me than my Lord, and He is nearer and dearer each day. I could never begin to tell what He has done for me. Almost every time I give my testimony, I hear of someone who has been helped, either physically or spiritually.

I praise God that He cares for all things that concern us. When the Lord told us to go to St. Paul, we had only two cents (Mrs. Monroe and I). After we told the Lord we would go, He gave us the fare. I had never heard of any such thing as trusting the Lord for financial aid until Mr. Bosworth told of his experiences. "Faith cometh by hearing, and hearing by the Word of God." One morning, we had thirteen cents; after getting a light breakfast, we had one cent left. So we cried out, shouting "glory" in the pocketbooks. (No one knew that we had gone on faith.) At the exact time that we did this, a special delivery letter was sent to us with two dollars in it. Three days later, when our rent was due, the Lord sent in fourteen dollars. That is the way He provided. When we were coming home, we had five dollars and twelve cents. I asked the Lord for my fare. By twelve that night (Saturday), He sent it in, and one dollar and eighty-five cents more.

I have had to rely on His promises for everything since, and He has never failed me. Use this testimony as you see fit—by the guidance of the Holy Spirit and all for the glory of God.

Mrs. Edith I. Watt Lau, Detroit, MI (This testimony was given a year after her healing.)

Healed of Cancer

About four years ago, a cancer started on my face. It was, at first, apparently only a small wart on my nose. I kept scratching it until it became a sore, and then it was apparent that a cancer had developed. At that time, I suffered very much, but before the second year, the pain and agony were extreme.

It was necessary to keep my face covered, both on account of its appearance and the necessity of keeping cloths saturated with ether and other aesthetics to check the pain. I spent about $500 for aesthetics during the last year I was sick. This was the only means of easing the suffering. When I removed the cloth, the pain was so intense that I was blinded and could not see my hand before my face.

I went from one physician to another in Ohio, Indiana, New York, and New Jersey, wherever I heard of a good one, looking for relief. I am sure I consulted more than fifty of them. But all of them said there was no hope and that they could do nothing for me.

But, praise the Lord, in September 1920, I heard of the Bosworth meetings that were being held in my hometown, Lima, Ohio. I went prompted by no other desire than to get healed. I had never heard the Gospel preached in this way before, and went forward immediately. When I was asked to pray, I did not know how, and the words had to be put into my mouth; but as I repeated them, faith came into my heart, and I began to be very happy.

They laid hands on me for healing, and as they did so, I could feel the power of God going through my body. It rose up into my face. The feeling was that of a tight rubber cap over my face that was being slipped off, little by little. When it reached the top of my head, I saw a bright light and I had a vision of Jesus standing right before me. Then I shouted in earnest, although I had not been able to do so before. As soon as the hands were laid on me, the pain ceased, and I knew I was healed. Others tell me I cried out, "I am saved and healed," and that I threw away the cloth that had covered my face. I was so happy that I was not aware of what I was doing. I shouted and shouted with joy, went home shouting, shouted almost all night, and continued shouting when I arose in the morning.

When I arose, my daughter had gotten breakfast. She looked at me and exclaimed, "Oh, Mother!" There was a big mirror in the dining room, and I looked in that. I saw that my upper lip, parts of which had been eaten away previously, was healed. It had been eaten away so that the roots of my teeth showed. During the night, it had filled in with new flesh, was covered with fresh skin, and was as solid and clear as it is at present. There were no traces left of the cancer except the scars. Two scabs that had been on my face were still there, but later disappeared. But wherever the skin had been gone, it was completely healed during the night and the new skin had formed.

My right thumb had been crippled for four years. My instep had been broken. They were both healed at the same time as the cancer. I have not had pain from either of them since that time.

When I saw that my lip was restored, I shouted so loud that the home soon filled up with neighbors, to whom I told the story of what God had done for me.

My children took my healing as an indication that the Lord would soon take me to heaven, and if I went out to the neighbors and stayed longer than I expected, they would come to see if I was still on the earth.

For two years, I had not been able to take anything except soup or milk. I could not open my mouth far enough to take food in, and had to sip liquid from a small spoon held to my lips. I was healed on Friday night, and on Saturday morning I took up knife and fork and began to eat just as I did before I was afflicted. When the

Bosworth brothers came to see me the same morning, I took a large tablespoon, opened my mouth wide, and showed them how I could eat. When they came, I was out visiting the neighbors and showing them my face, but they waited at my home until I returned and rejoiced with me over the healing.

On Sunday, I went out to be baptized. On Saturday, something had said to me, "Go into the water." Brother Bosworth explained to me what it meant, and I obeyed and was baptized.

On Monday, my daughter had a bushel of apples, and I sat peeling them and singing, "I know the Lord laid His hands on me; He healed the sick and raised the dead." I peeled the whole bushel before I realized that something had happened to my crippled hand. Then I found it was perfectly well.

As soon as the news of my healing spread, I had many callers asking for confirmation of it. I received letters from all over the world asking about it, and one day I received nineteen. I also had many out-of-town callers on the same errand. I was able to refer them to any of my neighbors about my previous condition, as all knew it. Three months ago, a doctor who had formerly prescribed for me came to my house. He asked me how I was getting along. I told him I was well and praising the Lord. He wanted to know what doctor I had. I told him, "Dr. Jesus." He said, "How long has he been here?" I answered, "As long as I have." He did not know that I meant the Lord Jesus Christ. When he understood, he shouted with laughter and was very happy over it. On Monday, after peeling the apples, I went and prayed for a woman who had cancer. She went to the meeting a night or two afterward and was healed. As I came out of her house praising the Lord, I passed the gas plant. The men working there asked me what the matter was. One of them must have been a Christian, for when I told them, he began to shout. Since my healing a year ago, I have not had any symptoms whatever of the cancer or any pain in my hand or foot; but about a month before coming to Toledo, I let a very large lump of coal fall on my foot. It was very badly bruised. Three or four days before I came here, a piece of bone about one-half inch long came out of it. After coming to Toledo, I was prayed for, and the foot healed.

There has been no pain in it since then.

Since I was saved, I have been called away many times to pray for the sick. In one case, it was a little boy, Billy Jones, who had been confined to his bed for several months. He was paralyzed and had bad sores on his back and face. I prayed for him and told the parents that in nine days he would walk. I said that because it seemed that a voice came to me with that message. In just nine days from that time, he walked to my house, two blocks away.

One day last winter, I was without coal. I knew that the Lord had promised to take care of me, so I prayed about it. On going downstairs, I found a lump of coal that filled a bushel basket when we broke it up. I never learned who sent it. When I pray for anything I need, I am sure to get it, just as if I had a friendly neighbor and she had given it to me. I do not always get it right away, but it comes nevertheless.

Just before I came to Toledo on this visit, I said to the Lord, "I would like to be in the Bosworth meetings once more." He immediately provided the money for me to go to Toledo. I knew I was going to a strange place, so I said, "Lord, I know you are going to take care of me." Through no effort of mine, He provided a beautiful place for me to stay while here.

When I had the cancer, I was obliged to sell my clothes to provide money for the ether, drugs, and other needs; so when I was healed, I was necessarily poor. But He has provided ever since. I have never wanted for a thing.

The first of April, last, we were exposed to the smallpox. The authorities quarantined us and would not provide for us. I prayed, and one day when we had run out of everything, there stood a man at the door with a great big basket of things. Both my daughter and I had a bad case of the disease but had no physician except Jesus, and came out all right, without any scars.

After nearly three years of suffering, to be instantly set free! It is almost too good to be true.

Mrs. Alice Baker, Lima, OH

Miss Lida Clark's Confirmation of Mrs. Alice Baker's Cancer Testimony

I was present at the time Mrs. Baker was healed of her cancer. After she had been anointed and prayed for, she said to someone, "Take that cloth off." The other person loosened it from her face, and Mrs. Baker took it and threw it away. She appeared to be just filled with the Holy Spirit. She cried out, "I am saved and healed," as she sprang to her feet. It could not have appeared to the audience that she was healed, any more than it did to me. Her face was a horrible sight. It was a mass of blood, pus, and open sores. But she said afterward that the pain had ceased and that she had the assurance in her heart that she was healed.

The odor from the cancer was so offensive that the worker who filled out her card was sick from it that evening and all the next day. But there was no odor the next night. I sat right alongside her and know that this was the case. And the cancer, the holes in her lip, and all the sores had disappeared. She was healed—that was undeniable.

After her healing, I saw a physician who had treated her during her illness. After hearing that she had been healed, he asked me to tell him what I had actually seen. I told him that I saw her come in with the cloth on her face, was present when she was prayed for, heard her say, as she took the cloth off, that she was healed, and saw her walk down the street without the cloth.

He said that it was impossible, that she could not have walked out without the cloth over her face because the pain would have been so intense as to have blinded her, and she could not have found her way out of the hall. He said, "Girl, you have been hypnotized; that could not be so."

I saw him again after he had seen her, and he said it certainly was a marvelous thing for her. He acknowledged it was so.

Miss Lida Clark, Lima, Ohio

Monster Cancer Healed

I visited Mrs. Trina Odegard of Woodstock, Illinois, in May of 1921, and was greatly surprised to see her in the condition in which I found her, more dead than alive. We knew that she had suffered from ulcers of the stomach for twenty-five years or more, and were of the opinion that she had cancer. Her meal consisted of a half slice of bread, and when I urged her to eat more, she told me that if she did, the pains would kill her. She was barely able to walk across the floor.

After I left, she consulted three physicians in Woodstock, had an x-ray photograph taken, and learned she had a serious case of cancer, far too advanced to even suggest an operation. The physicians gave as their opinion that she would never pull through. They gave her about two weeks to live. She decided to consult a specialist here in Chicago, and he told her the same thing. It was during this visit in July 1921 that she heard of the Bosworth tent meetings at Cicero and North Avenues. She was taken there at once, and when prayed for, was healed instantly. She said the power of God went down through her body from head to foot during the prayer.

Her soreness, pain, and suffering were gone instantly. The cancer was eliminated by the power of God. She was so hungry before leaving the tent that she could hardly wait until she got where she could get something to eat. She visited us the next day, ate the heartiest meal I had ever seen her eat in many a year, and there was not the slightest evidence of serious aftereffect.

It has been six months since her healing, and when I called her up the other evening, she was getting along fine. She has gained weight and is hungry all the time. The people in Woodstock were astonished, as they never expected to see her return alive after making the trip to Chicago.

It was through her wonderful healing that Mother and I were saved. We wanted to serve a God who was so loving, and we gave our hearts to Him right then and there. I am happier every day since I was converted.

These, however, are not all the blessings we received. I had been ailing and taking medicine for almost four years. I was so nervous that at times I almost went into hysterics. I was terribly anemic and also had internal trouble for which I had undergone an operation two-and-a-half years before. After that, I was worse than ever, not being able to gain weight or strength, whatever I did. I took nerve tonics, blood tonics, and serum injections. Nothing seemed to do me any good. I became disgusted with life, and decided to stop taking medicine.

I thank God that He led me to the Bosworth tent meetings, as I know He wanted me to go there so that He might save and heal me. I was not saved before that, and my healing came as soon as I gave myself to Jesus. I am gaining weight, am stronger than I have ever been, and am not nervous anymore. I also thank God for the perfect peace and joy that I have in my heart; and life with Christ is all joy and happiness.

Mother experienced a wonderful healing. One doctor said I had better see that she was taken care of immediately or I would not have her with me for very long. He said that she must have an operation for gall bladder and appendix trouble, as the pains were so severe she could not sleep. She had undergone an operation seven years ago and had not been well since. She had also suffered an abdominal rupture after returning home from the hospital, and so dreaded the thought of another operation. After being prayed for, she felt the power of God going through her, and she cried for joy. Her pains have left her entirely, and, praise the Lord, the rupture is being healed.

Mrs. R. Jerolaman, Chicago, IL

Cancer of the Leg Healed

I had suffered for years with a cancer on my leg. The pain caused me to tear my hair, and was too intense to describe. The doctors operated but brought no relief. For two years after the operation, I had not been able to lace my boot on account of the swelling, nor could I walk properly, kneel down, do my work, or go out. The cancer was pronounced a Melanotic Sarcoma. I had been confined to my bed continuously for four months.

Soon after being anointed and prayed with, the pain almost instantaneously left, and the swelling rapidly disappeared. The cancer has now completely gone, and only a few scars show where the black monster with its hideous head lived. The flesh has become pure and clean, and my health is perfect.

After being healed, I went to the doctor, who simply laughed and said, "Well, I am pleased to see it, Mrs. Killick, but I will bet you ten dollars it will be back in six months."

It is now nearly two years, and my condition is as described.

Mrs. Killick, Toronto

Multiple Healings

In October of 1921, I was healed by the power of God from cancer, sugar diabetes, enlargement of the heart, a twisted spine, almost total paralysis from the hips to the feet, the condition of being a nervous wreck, and almost total blindness. I had suffered from the cancer for one-and-a-half years, and from the other troubles for seven years. I walked only with crutches, and when I went out, it was in a wheelchair. A few weeks ago, the doctor who treated me said that I had been one of the greatest sufferers he had known.

About the twelfth of October, I had a bad spell and sent for the doctor. He said that I had about ten days to live, and no more. On October the fifteenth, a little man who was in the habit of bringing my newspaper came to the door and inquired as to my condition. He asked to see me and was granted permission with the suggestion that I undoubtedly would not recognize him. Before he went out, I knew him but was unable to speak.

He said, "Mrs. Killick, who has been healed of a terrible cancer, is coming here. Would you like to see her?" I nodded assent. She came to see me and told me that God wanted to heal me. She read the Bible to me and prayed, but I do not remember now what she said. She sang a hymn, and I do remember that. It was:

> Were the whole realm of nature mine,
>   That were a present far too small.
> Love, so amazing, so divine,
>   Demands my soul, my life, my all.

She departed, saying that she would come back again at night. I lay in bed thinking, and when my friend who was taking care of me came in, I said, "If God has healed that woman, He will heal me."

I asked the Lord what He would have me do, and I heard Him say plainly, "Put on your shoes and stockings." My friend said, "Dear, you cannot get up," but she brought the shoes and stockings. She lifted my foot to dress it, and I felt no difference, but the moment the stocking touched my foot, I felt the power of God touch my body. It started at my feet, just where I was obeying the command, and spread all over my body. I got up on my feet, although I had not stood alone for four years. Then I asked to have my clothes brought to me, and I dressed alone. I walked into the bedroom and did up my hair. My friend asked, "What are you going to do now?" I said that I was going to help her get supper. She asked me what I was going to eat, and I told her the same as she was. Previously, I had eaten only eggs and orange juice. I ate just what she ate.

I went to bed at nine and slept until six in the morning. I could not stay in bed, but got up, ate breakfast, washed the dishes, and asked God what He would like to have me do to glorify Him. I heard Him say, "Wax that floor." The Tempter said, "You cannot do that; you have not been on your knees for years." I waxed the floor from end to end, and Mrs. Killick saw it completed when she returned in the afternoon. She said, "I am going to give my testimony in the little Salvation Army Hall. Will you give yours?"

She offered to get an automobile to take me down, but I refused and walked all the way. When I reached there, the power of God so overcame me, I could not speak, and I remained but a few moments.

From that hour to this, God has given me strength and guided my steps. Last summer, I had charge of one of the largest summer homes of the Anglican Church, and often worked from six in the morning until two or three o'clock the next morning. I have been feeling perfectly well ever since my healing, except for an attack of pneumonia, from which the Lord delivered me without the aid of medicine or physician. My testimony has been a means of blessing to many, and some of the girls attending our own little Mission Hall, which I was led to open in faith, have been converted and healed through it.

Do you wonder that I love God? He has blessed me spiritually as well as physically, and I am sure I am the happiest woman on earth. Better than my own healing, He has used me mightily to tell others what He has done for me, and many have been wonderfully healed.

Miss R. Nix, Toronto

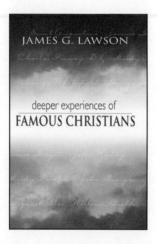

ANOTHER POWERFUL *B*OOK
from Whitaker House

Evening by Evening
Charles H. Spurgeon

In the quiet of the evening, God is ready to speak to your heart. Are you prepared to hear His voice? Combining Scripture with an inspiring and comforting message for each day, Charles Spurgeon shepherds you into intimate communication with the Father like you've never known before. Each evening you will find solace in God's Word.

ISBN: 0-88368-646-5 • Trade • 384 pages

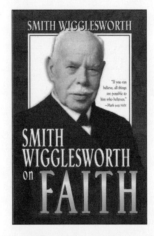

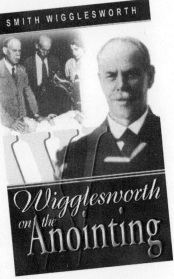